D0991282

ERRATA

The second sentence, line 3, of the Editors' Foreword, "Few had their works performed frequently during their lifetime; all have suffered from undeserved neglect," is not relevant to the life and career of the fifth composer in the series, Elinor Remick Warren. The career of this American composer, which continues today, is a long and distinguished one, as will be seen from a reading of this biography.

The Editors

Composers of North America

Series Editors: Sam Dennison, William C. Loring,
Margery Lowens, Ezra Schabas

ELINOR REMICK WARREN:

her life and her music

by
VIRGINIA BORTIN

Composers of North America, No. 5

The Scarecrow Press, Inc.
Metuchen, N.J., & London
1987

The author gratefully acknowledges all those who granted permission to reprint musical examples and excerpts from texts. Specific credits appear on page iii.

Library of Congress Cataloging-in-Publication Data

Bortin, Virginia.
    Elinor Remick Warren.

    (Composers of North America ; no. 5)
    Bibliography: p.
    Includes index.
    1. Warren, Elinor Remick, 1900-   .
2. Composers--United States--Biography. I. Title.
II. Series.
ML410.W2958B7 1987   780'.92'4 [B]   87-28357
ISBN 0-8108-2084-6

Copyright © 1987 by Virginia Bortin
Manufactured in the United States of America

Charles E. Wilson Library
Anderson University
Anderson, Indiana 46012

ML
410
.W2958
1987

Abram in Egypt. Copyright ©1962, 1978 by Carl Fischer, Inc., New York. Used by permission.
Along the Western Shore. Copyright © 1978 by Carl Fischer, Inc., New York. Used by permission.
The Crystal Lake. Copyright © 1978 by Carl Fischer, Inc., New York. Used by permission.
Easter Introit and *Christmas Introit* excerpts reprinted from *Praises and Prayers* (GE53) by Elinor Remick Warren. © Copyright 1982. General Words and Music Used with Permission 1987.
Good Morning, America! Copyright © 1976 by Carl Fischer, Inc., New York. Used by permission. Text from *Good Morning America!* copyright 1928, 1956 by Carl Sandburg. Reprinted by permission of Harcourt Brace Jovanovich, Inc.
The Harp Weaver. Copyright © 1932, 1978 by Carl Fischer, Inc., New York. Used by permission. Words by Edna St. Vincent Millay (from *The Ballad of the Harp Weaver*) published in *Collected Poems*, Harper & Row. Copyright © 1923, 1951, 1958 by Edna St. Vincent Millay and Norma Millay Ellis. Reprinted by permission.
Heather. Copyright ©1942 by Carl Fischer, Inc., New York. Used by permission.
If You Have Forgotten. Copyright © 1940 by Carl Fischer, Inc., New York. Used by permission. Words by Sara Teasdale, published by Macmillan.
The Legend of King Arthur. Copyright ©1939, 1974, 1978 by Carl Fischer, Inc., New York. Used by permission.
Little Choral Suite. Copyright © 1973 by Carl Fischer, Inc., New York. Used by permission. *A Little Song of Life* - words by Lizette Woodworth Reese (from *A Wayside Lute*) published by Holt Rinehart & Winston. *Sleep Walks Over the Hill* - words by Rowena Bastin Bennett (originally *Lady Sleep*) published by Follett.
Lonely Roads. Copyright © 1937 by Carl Fischer, Inc., New York. Used by permission. Words by John Masefield (from *Poems*), published by Macmillan.
My Heart is Ready. © MCMLXIX by the Lawson-Gould Music Publishers, Inc. Used by permission of the publisher.
The Night Will Never Stay. © MCMLXIV by the Lawson-Gould Music Publishers, Inc. Used by permission of the publisher.
Now Welcome, Summer! © 1984 by Lawson-Gould Music Publishers, Inc. Used by permission of the publisher.
On the Echoing Green. © 1987 by Lawson-Gould Music Publishers, Inc. Used by permission of the publisher.
Requiem. Copyright © 1965 by Carl Fischer, Inc., New York. Used by permission.
Singing Earth. Copyright © 1950, 1978 by Carl Fischer, Inc., New York. Used by permission. Texts for *The Wind Sings Welcome, Summer Stars,* and *Tawny Days* from *Smoke and Steel* by Carl Sandburg, copyright 1920 by Harcourt Brace Jovanovich, Inc.; renewed 1948 by Carl Sandburg. Reprinted by permission of Harcourt Brace Jovanovich, Inc. Text for *Great Memories* from *Good Morning, America!* copyright 1928, 1956 by Carl Sandburg. Reprinted by permission of Harcourt Brace Jovanovich, Inc.
Snow Towards Evening. ©1937, 1960 by G. Schirmer, Inc. Used by permission of the publisher.
Sonnets for Soprano and String Quartet. Copyright © 1974 by Carl Fischer, Inc., New York. Used by permission. Words by Edna St. Vincent Millay (from *Fatal Interview*) published in *Collected Poems*, Harper & Row. Copyright © 1931, 1951, 1958 by Edna St. Vincent Millay and Norma Millay Ellis. Reprinted by permission.
Suite for Orchestra. Copyright © 1978 by Carl Fischer, Inc., New York. Used by permission.
Symphony in One Movement. Copyright © 1978 by Carl Fischer, Inc., New York. Used by permission.
Transcontinental. Copyright © 1958, 1986 by Theodore Presser Co. Used By Permission Of The Publisher. Text of the poem *Transcontinental* by A.M. Sullivan originally published and copyrighted in 1941.
White Horses of the Sea. Copyright © 1932 by Carl Fischer, Inc., New York. Used by permission.
White Iris. Copyright © 1972 and 1979 by Theodore Presser Co., Bryn Mawr, PA. Used By Permission Of The Publisher.

Excerpt from *Two Tramps in Mud Time* by Robert Frost. Copyright 1936 by Robert Frost. Copyright © 1964 by Lesley Frost Ballantine. Copyright © 1969 by Holt, Rinehart and Winston. Reprinted from *The Poetry of Robert Frost* edited by Edward Connery Lathem, by permission of Henry Holt and Company, Inc.
Portions of the text of the Genesis Apocryphon as they appear in *Abram in Egypt* were adapted from a translation by Sulamith Schwartz Nardi and appear here with permission of the Shrine of the Book at Jerusalem.

Charles E. Wilson Library
Anderson University
Anderson, Indiana 46012-3462

CONTENTS

FOREWORD

Elinor Remick Warren is a distinguished American composer who has been writing songs, choral works and instrumental compositions for many years. Nearly 200 of these have been published, including a song which came from her pen when she was just a school girl in her teens.

Elinor Warren's music has been performed and heard in the two Americas, Europe and Asia. Because of her skill as a pianist, together with her compositional ability, she has acted as accompanist or has written songs for such artists as Lawrence Tibbett, Richard Crooks, Lucrezia Bori, and Nelson Eddy. Others who have included her songs on their recital programs are Kirsten Flagstad, Rose Bampton, Helen Traubel, Gladys Swarthout, and Lauritz Melchior.

This composer has not limited herself to choral and vocal compositions. During the 1930's Warren began to write for various instrumental combinations and full orchestra; her pieces appeared on the concert programs of such conductors as Alfred Wallenstein, John Barbirolli, Albert Coates, Wilfrid Pelletier, Andre Kostelanetz and Pierre Monteux. Her compositions have been played and sung in Athens, Vienna, and Jerusalem; two orchestral-choral concerts at the latter site and another at Caesarea brought to Israeli audiences the old story of Abram and Sarai with the text taken from the Book of Genesis and the Dead Sea Scrolls.

In writing the biography of Elinor Remick Warren, Virginia Bortin has recorded carefully each pertinent element in the life of the composer by alternating musical detail with frequent paragraphs describing family relationships which were unusually happy and affectionate. Such personal examples included the vacation days lived at the "Rancho Corona del Valle" located in the High Sierras, where husband Wayne Griffin spent time away from his business endeavors to raise champion quarter horses. Appearing in the biography are the accounts of Elinor's warm friendships with many of the great musical artists of our time; also, one may read a description of the manner by which each new composition was born and grew to reach its maturity in final form. There is the story of the daily sessions in Paris with Nadia Boulanger as a stern but marvelously gifted teacher; also, interesting and revealing episodes are found in the correspondence with the American poets Edna St. Vincent Millay, Robert Frost, and Carl Sandburg.

As is true of many composers, the scores of Elinor Warren show definite changes in their compositional style at various times. Virginia Bortin believes that these changes are particularly to be found in the works written after Warren's studies with Boulanger.

The biographer has provided the reader with detailed analyses of the more important scores. A catalog which carries much needed information concerning all of the published pieces is most helpful. Listed is the nature of each performing group, the authors of the several texts, publisher and date of publication, instrumentation or accompaniment, key, voice and range for vocal solos or choral pieces, etc.

One must commend Elinor Remick Warren for a successful career in a profession dominated almost exclusively by men. Further, such has been accomplished by a composer who has insisted that music and her family should enjoy equal importance in her expenditure of time, interest and affection.

This is a biography which paints the picture of a warm-hearted and gracious musician - loyal to family and friends, unafraid of hard work and inspired by and communicating to others the significance and beauty which is inherent in all great art.

Howard Swan

EDITORS' FOREWORD

This biographical series is designed to focus attention on significant North American composers from Colonial times until the present. Few had their works performed frequently during their lifetime; all have suffered from undeserved neglect.

Each volume consists of a substantial essay about the composer and a complete catalog of compositions. The essay deals with the composer's life and works in the context of the artistic thought and musical world of his or her time. Critical comments by contemporaries are included, as are illustrations and musical examples. Some works which merit performance today are singled out for analysis and discussion. The catalog of the composer's output has full publication details, locations of unpublished works and, where necessary, incipits.

We hope that this series will make its readers more conscious and appreciative of our North American musical heritage and serve as a guide to performing musicians seeking works of interest.

Sam Dennison
William C. Loring
Margery M. Lowens
Ezra Schabas

Series Editors

PREFACE

The music of Elinor Remick Warren first won my admiration more than thirty years ago when as a teenager I accompanied my cousin, a concert singer, in her favorite Warren songs. Many years later I sent the composer some of my poems, hoping she might like one of them well enough to honor me by setting it. Though not finding the poems suitable for her use, she graciously called to acknowledge my offering. That phone call was the start of a friendship which, combined with my regard of many years, has greatly enriched my life. Thus when Sam Dennison, editor of this series, approached me about writing a biography of Miss Warren, I did not hesitate.

This book has been four years in the making. The work has proceeded slowly because, while having had the benefit of being able to consult the subject on many matters of fact, I found that a large number of references in which she is profiled (including the venerable *New Grove Dictionary of American Music*) are riddled with inaccuracies. Further, outside Jane Weiner LePage's excellent and extensive chapter in *Women Composers, Conductors, and Musicians of the Twentieth Century*, there are no major biographical reference works extant.

Miss Warren's remarkable memory proved to be the foundation upon which I could erect the structure of this biography. However, all the facts of such a long and exceedingly active career could not be expected to be forthcoming from any one memory - even the subject's. Thus was I fortunate in having access to copyright documents, family memorabilia, scrapbooks, and copies of some of the composer's correspondence to and from friends, publishers, and fellow musicians, to substantiate and augment biographical information, as well as to modify errors of fact or perception. Moreover, I profited from the facilities of the UCLA Music Library and University Research Library. Here, I reviewed miles of microfilm, hunting down reviews and other articles not to be found among the composer's memorabilia. Interestingly, neither the Warren scrapbooks nor the UCLA microfilm archives produced many reviews that were less than complimentary. The widely scattered reference material yielded by this and other archives also helped greatly in rechecking information, as did my extensive interviews with the composer's family and friends.

A word about the *Discography*. I have here included both commercial and privately-obtained recordings of Warren works which are currently available at the New York Public Library and the Free Library of Philadelphia. Further, after an extensive survey of the major archival sources for recorded sound, as well as Miss Warren's own collection, I have been able to construct a list of many of the air checks of Warren works performed on radio over a number of years.

Since I did not have a publication date for every composition listed in the *Catalog of Works*, I thought it valuable, particularly in the case of manuscript material, to include the date upon which the work was completed, when such date could be ascertained by the composer and/or a variety of other sources. These sources included personal correspondence as well as articles in newspapers and periodicals.

I wish to thank the many persons who contributed valuable knowledge, advice and information to this book. Particular gratitude is due the children of Elinor Remick Warren - James Griffin, Wayne Griffin, Jr., and Elayne Techentin - who freely and charmingly offered their recollections and anecdotes. Friends and associates of the composer were also most generous in granting interviews: Rose Bampton, Roger Wagner, Howard Swan, Mildred Crooks, Sylvia Lee, Mona Bonelli, the late Betty Haldeman, James and Delphine Fahringer, Anne Perillo, Mildred Wohlford, and Esther Van Benscoten. Thanks also to the staffs of the Stanford University Archive of Recorded Sound, Yale University Library's Department of Historical Sound Recordings, the UCLA Music Library and University Research Library, and the New York Public Library's Rodgers & Hammerstein Archives of Recorded Sound. Special thanks also to Lance Bowling and to Professor Catherine Smith of the University of Nevada, Reno, for helpful comments and suggestions; and to my editor, Sam Dennison of the Edwin A. Fleisher Collection of Orchestral Music of the Free Library of Philadelphia.

Gratitude is also due Frances White Fry for the design
and composition of this volume.

Lastly, and certainly most importantly, I wish to acknowledge the debt I owe the composer herself, whose
patience in being interviewed over long hours was unflag-
ging, and who graciously opened her home, her files, and
her memories to almost daily intrusion over a period that
finally extended into years. It is my hope that this book
will add substantially to the reader's knowledge and appreciation of the contribution of Elinor Remick Warren, a
major figure in the musical history of our time.

Virginia Bortin
Los Angeles, California
April, 1987

1. PRELUDE AND YOUTH

On the night of March 21, 1940, Elinor Remick Warren stood on a Los Angeles concert stage, surrounded by members of the city's Philharmonic Orchestra, Oratorio Society, British conductor Albert Coates, and two soloists. An ovation greeted her. Her most ambitious work to date - one of the most ambitious of her life - had just been heard in its world premiere, the importance of which was underscored by the premiere's broadcast on nationwide radio over the Mutual Broadcasting System.

Repeatedly, she was brought back to the flower-laden stage to receive the cheers of her audience, to acknowledge the performers and the famed conductor who shared this triumph. Music critics mirrored the evening's enthusiasm, one of them writing she had "offered to music a classic of great depth and intrinsic worth."

This premiere of her choral symphony, *The Passing of King Arthur*, had already been the object of much national publicity. A major new composition by a beautiful young wife and mother had caught the fancy of Americans everywhere. A photograph of the composer feeding her infant son while correcting a score, dreamed up by an eager news photographer, had appeared in newspapers across the nation.

However, this performance marked no beginning for Elinor Remick Warren. Throughout the two previous decades, Warren works - piano solos, songs, choral and orchestral works - had been included in the catalogs of America's leading music publishers and performed by the world's greatest artists on concert stages in the United States and in Europe. As a pianist, Warren herself had performed with symphony orchestras, had given recitals, and toured as assisting artist with leading singers, who also programmed her songs. She had had her own weekly program on network radio and had made a series of commercial recordings of accompaniments for singers and concert pieces from her extensive repertoire. She was, in addition, happily married to a man successful in his own field, was a devoted mother and daughter, and the chateleine of a lively Los Angeles household. One is reminded of the young Clara Schumann, composer, pianist, wife of an eminent man, mother of a large family. Like Clara, Elinor Warren did not allow being a woman to deter her when seeking fulfillment in her field. Though newspaper articles of the period refer to her as one of the most successful of America's younger composers, they do not categorize her as a *woman* composer. Over the years, her work had held its own against competition from a musical establishment dominated by men and based in that unbreachable citadel, New York.

Though a handful of women, notably Amy Beach, Ruth Crawford Seeger, and Marion Bauer, - Easterners all - had preceded her, Elinor Remick Warren, during much of her career, stood virtually alone as a woman achieving renown in the world of American composition. Today, she has been joined by more women who have successfully entered the field. But for many years, no American composer of art songs, male or female, outdistanced her. And during the 1970's, a survey of major American symphony orchestras by *High Fidelity/Musical America* ranked her one of the most performed women orchestral composers of the decade.

How did a woman, living and working outside America's musical mainstream, manage to win out over the prejudices of critics, fellow musicians, and audiences? What are the wellsprings, the significant influences that went into the making of this unique career?

Elinor Remick Warren was the only child of parents whose roots reached far back into American history. Until she was ten, her family home was shared with a maternal great-grandfather, Leonard N. Harding, who had been a child while Thomas Jefferson still lived; whose life, he boasted to her, spanned both the invention of the match and of the airplane. She is a descendant, on her paternal side, of General Joseph Warren, an early patriot leader and the hero of Bunker Hill, at which battle he died in 1775.

Elinor's parents, of Scottish and Irish ancestry, were distantly related and had known each other since childhood. Her mother, Maude Remick, was born in Red Oak, near Des Moines, Iowa, but grew up in Pawnee, Nebraska, at a time when Indians could still cause fear among townspeople. She remembered being hidden, as a child, under the bed, when members of the local tribe would ride into Pawnee on their annual visit, stopping at the Remick house to ask for food. Young Maude had long, golden hair, and the Indians were rumored to kidnap blonde children, to raise them as their own.

In her teens, Maude Remick moved with her parents to Los Angeles, where her father, who had been one of the youngest of the Union Army generals in the Civil War, began buying up land. There, she became an accomplished pianist, studying with an older friend, a well-known concert pianist named Neally Stevens, who had been a pupil of Liszt. Maude Warren later told her daughter of having seen one of Liszt's used cigars, which her teacher kept enshrined as a souvenir of the great man.

Elinor's father, a native of Warren, Ohio, who grew up in Cleveland, received his name from James Garfield, a close family friend, long before Garfield became President of the United States. Originally the baby was named Clarence, but Garfield, on his first visit to view the infant, seemed hurt that his name had not been chosen. The baby was renamed on the spot, and the future President promised, "When he's a young man I'll see that he has a good start in life." An assassin's bullet tragically cut short that pledge.

James Warren, who had hoped to be a professional singer, had studied voice in his youth and possessed a fine tenor. A man of wit, with an outgoing, gregarious nature, Warren later recalled he was forced to propose many times before his intended bride, twelve years younger, would consent to marry him. After their wedding in 1895, at the Remick home in Los Angeles, the couple returned to Cleveland, where Warren had established himself in banking after giving up the idea of a career in music. But the harsh Ohio winters proved devastating for his fragile young bride, and Warren made the decision to forego his banking career and return to Los Angeles. There he and a partner established Warren and Bailey Manufacturing Company which, in those early days of the town's rise, quickly became a success. General David Remick built his daughter and her husband a comfortable house at 9th and Alvarado, near MacArthur Park - originally Westlake Park. When he died a few years later, General Remick left the young couple his extensive real estate holdings.

The Warrens' only child, Elinor, was born shortly after the century's turn, on George Frederick Handel's birthday, February 23. During the first years of her life, not understanding why she could not share her mother's birthday, which fell on Chopin's natal date, six days later, the child would protest that she wanted her own birthday included in her mother's festivities. A gentle woman, subject to severe headaches and disliking dissension of any kind, Maude Warren decided they must celebrate together, on March 1. Not until the age of nine did Elinor finally discover the loving deception.

In addition to her great-grandfather, also sharing the Warren home during Elinor's formative years was her maternal grandmother. Mildred Wohlford, a close friend throughout Elinor's life, remembers this grandmother, Sarah Jane Remick, as being an extremely lovable, outgoing person. Wohlford's early impressions of Elinor's mother were that she seemed somewhat stiff and quiet, though later she was to observe Mrs. Warren's warmth and sense of humor. Elinor's father she remembers as being very protective of family and friends.

The composer recalls that all four adults, each in his or her own way, offered her much affection as she was growing up. But, though a great deal of attention was focused on Elinor, the adult members of the family were determined she would not become a "spoiled only child," and strict discipline reigned alongside loving attention. Much fun was generated by Elinor's jovial father, who in later life admitted he had a hard time not indulging his little girl. Though devoting his adult life to business, James Warren never lost interest in music, especially vocal music. With his wife at the piano, he spent many evenings singing in the family music room and was in charge of music for the Sunday School at his church. Elinor was taken to Sunday School every week and can remember her father leading the singing there, his strong, clear tenor standing out against all the other voices. Elinor's "Nana," Sarah Remick, became the child's roommate on family trips - especially during a seven-month visit to Europe when Elinor was twelve, in the course of which the composer recalls hearing Wagner's entire "Ring" cycle in Munich and more opera in Dresden.

Surrounded by adults, Elinor sometimes chafed at being an only child. Two months before her fourth Christmas, she requested that Santa bring her a brother, a sister, or a puppy. She received the puppy, a black cocker which she still remembers loving with possessive devotion. However, the solitude imposed upon an only child living among older people must have been useful in preparing her for the many hours she would later be required to spend alone in the pursuit of her craft.

Believing from the first that her granddaughter was destined to accomplish great things in music, on the eve of Elinor's fifth birthday Sarah Remick suggested she have a photograph taken. The following day she was to take her first music lesson. "Nana" wanted the photograph "so you will always remember this event."

Sarah Remick's intentions were not without basis. Since the age of three, Elinor had been picking out pieces on the piano, which her mother copied into notebooks. These miniature compositions were written either as piano solos or as songs, for which the child also wrote lyrics and full piano accompaniments. Sometimes composed to celebrate a special occasion, each piece is carefully dedicated to an adult of significance in its creator's life. Some years later, pianist Harold Bauer, examining these early notebooks, expressed surprise that so young a child, lacking formal musical training, would have composed in correct form.

In part, this can be explained by the fact that Elinor spent her formative years in a musical household. Her earliest memory is of her mother playing the piano; she can also recall the excitement of sneaking out of bed to sit quietly on the landing and listen in the evenings as her parents played and sang. The composer remembers

that from her earliest years she was excited by sound -
and not just musical sound. At the age of five, she would
accompany her parents to their summer cottage near the
beach at Venice, California. There, at night, she would
wake up and listen to the breakers outside her window.
She was thrilled by the sound of the waves building up,
moving in, and finally crashing on the shore. For her, this
represented a kind of aural "fireworks," as magical as any
Fourth of July sky-show.

At the turn of the century, Los Angeles had already
become a mecca for people of many different national-
ities. Germans, English, Chinese, and Canadians began
arriving in great numbers. Though in 1900 the population
had been 102,479, by 1920 it had burgeoned to 319,198.
The city's musical life grew with its expanding population.
Even before the new century had dawned, on October 14,
1897, Los Angeles had been the scene of a musical event
of international significance: the first North American
performance of a new opera by the young Giacomo
Puccini, presented by the Del Conte Grand Opera Company of Turin, Italy. It was called *La Boheme*. Until 1919,
orchestra concerts were given by the Los Angeles Symphony Orchestra, under the baton of Harley Hamilton, and
later Adolf Tandler, whose afternoon performance series
young Elinor regularly attended with her mother and
grandmother. In 1919, philanthropist William Andrews
Clark, Jr., a fine amateur violinist, founded a rival
orchestra, which he named the Los Angeles Philharmonic.
Walter Henry Rothwell was its first conductor. Clark contributed $100,000 annually to support the orchestra and
hired first chair players from orchestras in the East.

The rapid growth in population made Los Angeles a
natural stop-over point for concert and opera stars on
their national tours. During this first decade of the
twentieth century, America still clung to roots both
European and Romantic. Elinor's early visits to Simpson's
Auditorium for recitals given by the great musicians of
the day, and hours spent listening to her parents' Victor
phonograph guided her toward the neo-Romantic style
which she has followed during much of her career. Many
of those first recitals she heard were vocal, as were the
records to which she listened at home, along with her

parents' music-making and her father's Sunday School
singing. From her earliest years the composer can
remember wanting to sing, as did her father. Thus, not
only were the roots of her musical experience European
and Romantic, they were vocal as well.

Elinor's first "vocal teacher" was the family coachman, Oscar McLean. The Warrens kept two horses, as well
as a cow for fresh milk. As a small child, Elinor would be
allowed to ride each morning on the back of the cow,
whose name was Cherry, while Oscar led it to a vacant
lot to graze for the day. Then in the evenings she would
go back to the pasture with Oscar and sit astride Cherry
as the cow was led home to the barn. On one of these
outings she began humming a tune. The coachman decided
he must teach her some songs. After a time of serious
practice, Elinor had learned the first of Oscar's songs and
he proudly sent her into the house, where she proceeded
to startle her unsuspecting parents with a lusty rendition
of *Rufus, Rastus, Robinson Brown* - all the words of which
she still can recall.

When the time came to choose a piano teacher for
their musically precocious child, Maude and James Warren
chose well. Kathryn Montreville Cocke had begun her
career teaching kindergarten, but a dozen years later
decided to concentrate on musical instruction, using a
method devised by Mrs. Fletcher Copp, a pedagogue who
applied the principles of kindergarten teaching to music.

Recently reading Nancy B. Reich's biography of Clara
Schumann, Elinor Warren was surprised to learn that the
great 19th century musician had received training virtually
identical to her own. Clara Schumann's father, Friedrich
Wieck, greatly admired the method of a music teacher
born in Germany but trained in England, Johann Bernhard
Logier, and he primarily used Logier's system to train his
daughter. Had the Fletcher Method been a direct
"borrowing" of this earlier European system? Both con-
cepts, according to Warren, taught the notes from the
beginning, Kathryn Cocke's version giving them names such
as "Apples A", "Babies B." Moreover, before students did
any work at the piano, they must know the scales in
every key, as well as the major and minor triads and the
dominant 7th and 9th chords with inversions in all keys.

At the same time, they were given ear training, learning
early to recognize chords and notes away from the piano.
Kathryn Cocke believed that relative pitch could be
developed in anyone; it was simply a matter of training.
Young Elinor, however, was found to have absolute pitch.

Though not an accomplished pianist herself, Kathryn
Cocke was a thorough musician, a painstaking disciplinarian and an enlightened teacher. Five-year-old Elinor was
given two lessons a week with Miss Cocke or with one of
her pianist-assistants, as well as a Saturday morning group
lesson at which the children learned principles of music
through supervised musical games. The composer can recall
learning about "Mrs. Treble Clef and Mr. Bass Clef - the
two dots being his cuff buttons, the notes being their
children."

During their first year, students had no lessons at the
piano, but were taught to read music, to understand
rudimentary harmony, as well as the most intricate
rhythmic patterns. By the time they finally set hands to
keys, they knew all the principles, taught largely through
games. However, some of these musical drills were hardly
play. At the Saturday group lessons, students would be
required to stand at a blackboard upon which were
written lines of notes of various time denominations, from
whole notes up to 64th notes, with no divisions for the
measures. After the teacher indicated a time signature,
the pupil must mark those divisions in the proper places.
In this way, while still very young children, Elinor and
her classmates thoroughly learned to sight read the most
complex time values. By the time she had reached the age
of twelve, Elinor could play a Bach fugue, instantly
transposing it, upon command, into any key. Later asked
how she did it, the composer responded, "I think we just
didn't dare not to."

Throughout Elinor's instruction with Miss Cocke, study
of harmony and theory was incorporated into her weekly
lessons. Soon she had advanced to a point where, once a
week, she would have a lesson with one of her teacher's
assistants, young pianists just returned from study in
Europe and possessing far greater technical ability and
performing experience than the teacher herself.

Warren remembers Kathryn Cocke as a strict but loving disciplinarian who would rap knuckles with a ruler
when displeased. In the case of one recalcitrant student,
the teacher would call her house every morning at six
o'clock to be sure she got up in time to practice before
going to school. Such diligence was not lost on the
youngsters in her classes. One of them, comparing her
with a teaching assistant, said, "Miss S. makes you play
as well as you *can*; Miss Cocke makes you play *better*
than you can!"

Esther Van Benschoten, who, as Esther Church,
attended Miss Cocke's classes with Elinor, recalls the
teacher as being a very dominating but inspirational person, who managed to know many of the important
musicians of the day. When she thought a child had
talent, she gave unstintingly of her time and energy in
the development of that talent. Esther had small hands
that could not reach the octave; each morning Miss Cocke
would go to her house and massage her hands, hoping
somehow to improve the child's reach.

Though stern with many of her pupils, with Elinor,
Kathryn Cocke adopted quite another approach. Finding
the child to be a charming and beautiful, but painfully
shy little girl, who often would break into tears when
someone unfamiliar addressed her, the teacher quickly
devised a means of reaching the sensitive youngster. She
gave her a large, beautifully dressed doll, which Elinor
promptly christened Kate, for her teacher. Now the little
girl had found a non-threatening object to whom she could
address the answers to her teacher's musical questions;
for whom she could play her pieces.

Today, Warren credits Kathryn Cocke with saving her
from the emotional problems that could have arisen had
not "Kate" eased her past her shyness. Years later, Nadia
Boulanger was also to praise the remarkable Los Angeles
teacher for offering Warren, during her childhood years,
an unusually solid foundation, missing in many of the
students - far more mature and experienced – she
encountered at Fontainebleau.

Important musicians of the day were invited by
Kathryn Cocke to listen to and give their advice con-

cerning some of her most advanced pupils. By the age of
eight Elinor had reached that category, and she began
taking a lesson each month with Herr Thilo Becker, a
well-known German pianist and teacher, who was a friend
of Paderewski. With Becker, she made her first significant
public appearance at Simpson's Auditorium, in Miss
Cocke's students' recital, playing Mozart's *Sonata in C* (K
545), Becker playing Grieg's second piano part. Far from
being overwhelmed, the eight-year-old found the experience exhilarating; she had learned in one heady moment
that shyness need not interfere with performing. In fact,
when the audience began applauding, the little girl completely forgot Herr Becker and kept bowing until
prompted from the wings to acknowledge her distinguished
partner.

Among Kathryn Cocke's celebrated assistants with
whom young Elinor later studied was Olga Steeb. A Los
Angeles native, Steeb had become famous overnight when,
in 1911 in Berlin, she had played, at the age of 19, nine
major concertos in two weeks of appearances with the
Berlin Philharmonic. Back in her home town, too, she had
created a sensation; it was said she could play all the
keyboard works of Bach and 400 other compositions as
well. Elinor recalls being present when, at a dinner party
in her parents' home, philanthropist William Andrews
Clark, Jr., who had just pledged his annual contribution of
$100,000 to maintain the brand-new Los Angeles Philhar-
monic, told Steeb that one reason he had given the gift
and founded the musical organization was that "now you
will be able to play very often right here with our
orchestra."

In between concert appearances throughout the world,
Olga Steeb would give Elinor a lesson once each week.
Later, when Warren herself had become a concert artist,
she would occasionally prepare for various engagements by
having a session of coaching with Steeb.

Though her father feared that too much piano practice would not be healthy for his daughter, Elinor's
mother arranged for the child to be excused early from
school each day, in order to devote part of the afternoon
to her music. A talented, creative woman, Maude Warren,
in addition to her own pianistic ability, played the Irish

harp, made beautiful book-bindings and, when the Warrens decided to build a summer house by the sea in Venice, California, drew up the architectural plans for it.

Elinor adored her mother. She has retained throughout her life a vivid childhood memory of Maude Warren, standing in the kitchen in the morning, skimming cream from Cherry the cow's milk. She was wearing a light summer dress and the sun streamed through the window on her golden hair. Watching from the doorway, the child thought her mother the most beautiful person she had ever seen, and this image impressed itself deeply upon her.

Understanding the pitfalls to which young pianists are prone, Maude Warren sat with her daughter through each daily practice session, gently correcting, allowing no bad habits to creep into her playing, and preventing her from practicing mistakes. Years later, after achieving world recognition as a musician, Elinor Warren paid tribute to her mother's devotion, binding into several beautifully-tooled leather volumes her published works, with this inscription: "To Mama, remembering all the hours spent by a little girl's side at the piano, so long ago, which was the beginning of the making of these pieces."

Though practicing the piano daily and fast developing into a skilled pianist, the budding musician continued composing pieces on her own, her mother lovingly copying them into notebooks, "to save Elinor's eyes."

Esther Van Benschoten recalls that though there were a number of youthful talents in Miss Cocke's classes, Elinor outdistanced them all. "She had a depth that was far beyond the rest of us," she remembers. "We regarded her as the prodigy." However, Miss Cocke did not want any of her more talented students to become self-important about their successes. "Don't feel proud if you are playing well," she enjoyed reminding them. "Remember, your talent is a gift from God and you have to use it with the right attitude."

The year she was eight, Elinor learned she would be permitted to stay up late to attend a recital given by her idol, Ignace Jan Paderewski, who had included Los Angeles on his national concert tour. She had just learned his

Minuet in G and hoped to hear the great man play it. When she mentioned this to her teacher, Kathryn Cocke suggested that as he had not performed the piece in recital for many years Elinor should write him a letter requesting it. One morning after Sunday School, the youngster, sitting on Miss Cocke's front steps, composed a letter telling Paderewski what it would mean to be allowed to stay up late to hear him play the *Minuet* for her.

The night of the concert, convinced she would be favored with the piece, Elinor sat spellbound, listening to her musical god. Overflow patrons were seated onstage, which seemed to bother the Polish virtuoso. Looking as if he wanted to get away, he played one encore. Though the audience kept applauding, he did not reappear, and the Warrens bundled up their disappointed child to return home.

Several days later, a letter arrived for Elinor from Paderewski's manager. Thanking her for her letter, the man explained the pianist had agreed in advance he would play his composition "for the little girl." But, bothered by the crowd onstage, he had forgotten. As they were about to leave the auditorium for their train, the manager asked Paderewski why he had forgotten the *Minuet*. Whereupon the pianist threw off his coat, dashed onstage again and played it. But by this time "the little girl" was on her way home. The manager ended his letter by saying, "He [Paderewski] seemed to hear your little hands clapping with appreciation."

Beginning with the primary grades and continuing through high school, Elinor attended the Westlake School for Girls, still one of Los Angeles's finest preparatory schools. Perceiving they had a student of exceptional talent, the school's two headmistresses permitted the young musician to go home each day at one, to spend the first part of the afternoon practicing, after which she played with neighbor children. At Westlake, Elinor particularly enjoyed her classes in drama, often appearing as the lead in school plays. There, also, she nurtured the love of poetry which had already been stimulated by her mother's bedtime readings from the great poets. Mildred Wohlford, who, as Mildred Finley, was her classmate there, recalls that Elinor had a marvelous scholastic record, being one of the three top students in her class. She was also much loved. In her senior class yearbook is a charming picture of the young girl, beside it a quotation from Robert Burns, chosen by her classmates to exemplify their feelings: "Elinor Warren - 'But to see her was to love her, Love but her and love forever.'"

That same yearbook contains three pieces of writing by the teenage Elinor: a graceful sonnet, and two short narratives, one describing Venice, Italy, the other, an Alpine village; she had visited both during her European sojourn several years before. The descriptions of these places - obviously meaningful to the impressionable girl - are sensitive and vivid. Reading them, it is easy to understand the importance that word pictures play in some of her musical output. Besides poetry and narratives, the Westlake Yearbook for 1918 also reproduces two of Elinor's early songs.

Literary interests and pursuits vied with music for the child's attention from her earliest years. At the family dinner-table each evening, she would beg to be excused early (she always finished ahead of everyone else) to "go write my novel." At age eleven she had embarked upon a series of novels, of which she managed to complete several.

In the Warren household, seated around the table at every meal would be four generations: Elinor, her father and mother, her maternal grandmother and the great-grandfather who had lived through much of the 19th century. The latter had been a lifelong friend of the child's grandfather, General David Remick who, thirty years older than his wife, Elinor's much-loved "Nana," had died at the turn of the century.

As a young child, Elinor would accompany her mother on alternate Fridays as she would "go calling" at the homes of various women friends. On the other Fridays, the friends would come to the Warrens' for tea and conversation. Elinor was always permitted to sit quietly and listen while the grown-ups talked.

The wide age spread in her household - all of whose members but she had reached their maturity in the last

century and held to conventions of a different era - plus
the grown-up conversations of her mother's friends - gave
the only child a mature perception and inner discernment
she might otherwise not have expressed so early. It
further bred in her the impulse toward neo-Romanticism
which she would follow throughout most of her creative
life.

It was for a Westlake production that Elinor wrote
the first song she would see in print. During her junior
year, she starred in a production of Madeleine Lucette
Ryley's romantic comedy, *Mice and Men*, for which she
composed a setting of the poem by Robert Burns, *My Love
Is Like a Red, Red Rose*. Her father had it printed privately for use by the performers.

The Warrens had not long to wait, however, before
their daughter's ability gained her a legitimate publisher.
While still at Westlake, a hand injury forced her to focus
on composing, after some years spent away from it.
Though she had early and continuously written small
pieces, at the age of ten she abruptly stopped doing so.
This resulted from a conversation between her parents
which she accidentally overheard. Her father commented
on a recent song his daughter had written, stating it
seemed so mature, Elinor must have heard it somewhere
and unconsciously remembered it. His wife agreed. The
youngster was hurt and angry that the two persons she
loved most should question her integrity; without any
explanations she stopped composing. Not until high school
and her wrist injury did she start in again with serious
intentions.

The ironically fortunate mishap occurred when Elinor
was fifteen; while knitting a sweater, she pulled a
ligament in her right wrist, which had to be strapped for
several months. Though this curtailed piano practice, she
could still use the hand to write and during this period
began lessons in composition with Gertrude Ross, the
noted pianist-composer. Ross had toured as accompanist
for Mme. Schumann-Heink, who scored a great success
with Ross's song, *Dawn on the Desert*.

Ross encouraged Elinor to submit one of her compositions, *A Song of June*, to G. Schirmer, a leading New

York publisher. Schirmer accepted the song, sending the teenager her first contract.

A *Song of June*, dedicated to a school friend, was set to a poem by Bliss Carman, which presents a view of life and its beauty which has remained significant in Warren's work:

> Over the shoulders and slopes of the dune
> I saw the white daisies go down to the sea,
> A host in the sunshine, an army in June,
> The people God sends us to set our hearts
>   free.
> The bobolinks rallied them up from the dell,
> The orioles whistled them out of the wood;
> And all of their saying was, "Earth, it is
>   well!"
> And all of their dancing was, "Life, thou art
>   good!"

Though she sold this first song outright for the sum of fifteen dollars, Elinor Warren from now on could claim to be a published composer and thereafter merit any publisher's standard royalty. With this first check she opened a savings account, optimistically titling it "music earnings." It was a proud day when, with money from this account, she later bought the Steinway she plays today.

Gertrude Ross encouraged her young student to send more songs to publishers. She also suggested that Elinor accept an invitation to join the Dominant Club, a Los Angeles organization of professional women musicians. Elected just after finishing high school, she became the youngest member ever to be invited into the prestigious organization, which she later served as president and of which she is now an honorary member.

During the first half of the century, Los Angeles could boast many musical organizations such as the Dominant and MacDowell Clubs, which offered monthly musical programs given by the city's leading musicians for members and their guests. Elinor appeared frequently on these programs, sometimes playing a piano recital of works by other composers; often presenting - with soloists of her choosing - groups of her own vocal works.

At one such performance of her songs which she gave while still in high school, she met the eminent American composer Charles Wakefield Cadman. Organist, music critic, conductor and pianist, as well as composer, Cadman had studied and composed largely on themes of American Indian music. His songs *From the Land of the Sky Blue Water* and *At Dawning* had won him lasting recognition. Though also a serious composer of suites, symphonic poems and cantatas, he is best remembered for his music relating to the American Indian.

Cadman, sharing the program with Elinor, who was twenty years his junior, advised her to keep on writing and to let nothing deter her, further predicting that she would have a great career as a composer. He closely followed her career until his death in 1946, writing long letters of helpful advice which he would sign "Uncle Charlie Cadman." Cadman was the first of many eminent musical figures with whom Elinor Warren would be associated in the years which lay before her.

For her final year in high school, Elinor was anxious to have the experience of living at Westlake with her friends. She became a boarding student at the school, which was located within walking distance of the Warrens' house.

Following graduation, the young musician spent a year at home in advanced studies with Gertrude Ross and Olga Steeb. However, most of her friends had gone on to college, and finally she decided this was the route for her as well.

Her close friends of this period have remarked upon the fact that Elinor was given less freedom than many of her peers. She did not date a great deal and looked several years younger than her age. Further, her parents were exceptionally protective. Mildred Wohlford recalls a party to which both she and Elinor were invited during this time. Mildred's brother was Elinor's date and planned on driving her to the party at a house located in Bel Air, up a winding road. Though Mildred's brother was a good driver, the day before the party Elinor's father drove the road in his own car, to be sure it was safe for his daughter.

A dutiful and faithful person toward those she loves, Elinor is, nonetheless, strong-willed. At crucial points in her life, she has taken charge and made the decisions for herself that she considered necessary. Now, she decided upon Mills College in Oakland, California, as the logical next step for her life and work. Though her first choice had been Stanford, which many of her friends attended, the university at that time did not have a strong music department. Mills, then as now, was renowned for its music program. Her friend Mildred transferred to Mills from Stanford and became her roommate.

Elinor relished her college experience, including the occasional weekend house-parties and other social activities, in what for her was a new-found freedom. However, her musical knowledge had developed far beyond that of

Charles E. Wilson Library
Anderson University
Anderson, Indiana 46012-3462

her fellow students and what the school at that time could offer. Eventually, she became restless; New York, mecca of all serious musicians, beckoned.

Mills president Dr. Aurelia Reinhardt, an enlightened educator, was aware that the young woman had already fulfilled her musical requirements at a much earlier age, and that she needed only two years to complete the school's academic requirements. She urged Elinor to stay on a second year, whereupon she would be graduated.

But, encouraged by a member of the voice faculty, who also realized New York was where her student should be, Elinor could not be persuaded to stay beyond the freshman year, which she completed. That year did not prove unproductive. Elinor continued writing songs, sometimes stealing time to compose from the allotted piano practice period. Though she did not possess the natural equipment essential to the successful singer, the composer nonetheless studied singing at Mills in order to understand more about the limitations and possibilities of the human voice and to acquire the knowledge of vocal repertoire which she knew would be necessary to her work. Moreover, she was frequently invited to informal teas in Dr. Reinhardt's home, where the president would read poetry for her guests. Warren recalls these gatherings as a highlight of her college days. Dr. Reinhardt read poetry masterfully, offering the impressionable student a fresh awareness of the cadence and beauty of this form of expression.

The Warrens were extremely reluctant to remove their only child from a fine college and send her off to New York. They had heard "wild tales about musicians" and argued that their daughter could be just as successful composing at home. But Elinor thought differently. Though generally softspoken and possessed of a puckish sense of humor, she can be fiercely determined regarding matters she considers important to her life and the lives of those she loves. She admires such strength of purpose in others, as well, and likes to illustrate with a story about her friend, the late Metropolitan Opera singer, Ruth Chamlee. While walking with her father as a very young child, Chamlee slipped off the curb into the street, covering her new white dress with mud and scraping her knees. The child's father stood by, watching her struggle to right herself. When chided by passersby for not helping his daughter, he answered firmly, "The little girl will pick herself up!" How glad she was, said Ruth Chamlee in later years, that she could remember her father's words, for the future brought times when she *had* to "pick herself up."

Warren's creative temperament, which can display Herculean patience with anything involving her music, grows quickly impatient when faced for any extended period with matters unworthy of her time or effort. Now, in deciding whether or not to spend another year at Mills, she again faced a turning-point. But this combination of determination and impatience to get on with the career she had chosen prevailed; soon the young composer left Los Angeles, where her life had been remarkably sheltered, to descend upon New York. In her suitcase she carried a sheaf of new songs and choruses.

Her apprehensive parents came with her to settle her in an apartment they had rented on West 67th Street. They had arranged for her to share it with a Los Angeles friend who was to study singing. Warren had decided upon her New York teachers: for accompanying and song repertoire, the celebrated singing coach and accompanist Frank LaForge; and for orchestration, counterpoint and the larger forms, Dr. Clarence Dickinson, renowned composer and organist at the Brick Presbyterian Church on Park Avenue.

Dickinson, also director of the School of Sacred Music at Union Theological Seminary, greatly influenced church music in the twentieth century. Elinor had written him saying she wished to become his pupil, but had received no answer. Immediately after arriving, she went to the Brick Church and stationed herself on the steps of the organ loft until Dickinson had finished playing a concert. She begged him to accept her. Wanting no more pupils, Dickinson hesitated but, perceiving her zeal, reluctantly said yes.

This marked the beginning of a long friendship with Dickinson and his wife Helen. During these years in New York, they frequently invited the young Californian to spend weekends with them at their house in Hastings-on-Hudson. Warren remembers Clarence Dickinson as being a kind, almost saintly man, with a great reputation in New York and much influence with publishers. He took many of her compositions to his publisher, H.W. Gray, and through his recommendations she began a long association with this firm.

Warren had admired Frank LaForge since childhood; it had been he, more than anyone else, who turned accompanying into a true art form. He was also a celebrated composer. She had often heard LaForge when he came to Los Angeles to play for leading opera and concert artists, always accompanying them without music. It had been her dream to study with him, to learn all he knew about the voice and interpretation of the vocal literature. In addition to her work with him, LaForge suggested Ernesto Berumen for piano studies. At that time, Berumen was one of the city's most celebrated teachers.

LaForge enjoyed giving small dinner parties for his students from distant places, helping to make them feel at home and a part of the New York scene. During these evenings he would tell hilarious stories about the musical celebrities with whom he had worked.

LaForge took a great personal interest in his students. This prompted Elinor, one day, to bring him one of her songs, *The Heart of a Rose*, set to a poem by Alfred Noyes, for his critical comments. After she had played and sung it, LaForge looked astonished. "How did a little girl like you set music to such a profound and spiritual poem as this?" Realizing her talent, he suggested she show some of her songs to the renowned singers who worked with him. When she protested her singing voice was not good enough to "audition" the songs for such important artists, he smiled. "Don't worry about that. Just tell them you have a 'composer's voice.'" She never forgot his advice; in fact, the only persons who have heard what she refers to as her "bass-baritone" singing voice are great singers; for them she performs unashamedly, remembering LaForge's words.

Soprano Rose Bampton recalls her first encounter with Warren's "composer's voice": "When Elinor came to my

apartment bringing some of her songs for me to hear, I
watched this slight little girl begin the accompaniment,
playing with a gorgeous tone. She was so beautiful and
full of life. Then she sang, and I was astounded at this
deep voice she had. But the songs were beautiful!"

New York during these years was a hotbed of revolutionary musical activity. The upheavals of World War I
had marked a final break with 19th century traditions and
conventions. A new spirit of pessimism and futility had
invaded the arts. In Europe, Arnold Schoenberg - whose
Los Angeles lectures, held for composers, Warren would
later attend - had utilized atonality in his three
Klavierstuecke, Op. 11, and a musical theorist, Richard H.
Stein, had devised a system of composition using quarter
instead of half-tones. Now, many American musicians
became swept up in the wave of experimentation. The
United States, beginning to achieve its own reputation on
the international musical scene, welcomed the extremists
from Europe. At the time Elinor Warren arrived in New
York, both Ernst Bloch and Edgar Varèse were teaching
and working there. Warren has speculated on how her
musical style could have been altered had she been
directed to study with teachers involved in the new
music. However, she believes she might still have pursued
the course she did, as she is by nature no revolutionary.

Regardless, the young composer found herself stimulated by the creative winds sweeping Manhattan and
began writing at a fast pace. Upon finishing a new song,
she would sometimes go to a publisher's office to play
and "sing" it in person. Leading music publishers - Carl
Fischer, Theodore Presser, G. Schirmer - readily offered
her contracts for most of her songs. Today, these same
publishers are among those who still include her in their
catalogs.

During the four and a half years she spent in New
York, Elinor worked ceaselessly at her music - both composition and piano. Between weekly lessons in piano,
accompanying, and composition, as well as hours of daily
piano practice, she spent every moment composing - the
latter often cutting into her self-allotted sessions for
piano practice. She recalls that at this time, when finding
herself stuck upon a musical problem, she would often put

the manuscript under her pillow at night, amused to find that next morning the problem seemed to have been solved.

Largely due to Dickinson's influence, Warren now began writing more for chorus. Up to 1921 and her New York sojourn, she had mainly written songs and piano solos. Now she moved into a field of composition that would enlarge her musical perception and prove a mainstay of her professional life. The new direction is not surprising; she had been listening to choral music since her teens. Her father had, for a few years, been president of Los Angeles's Orpheus Club, a men's choral group. During his tenure with the organization, Elinor regularly attended its concerts and went to occasional rehearsals, which offered her an introduction to the techniques of choral composition.

In New York, under the tutelage of Dickinson, one of America's well-known composers of choral and organ music, she wrote many sacred compositions for chorus, with organ or piano, which were published and sung extensively. But at the same time she wanted to add secular choral pieces to her catalog; publishers also welcomed these. During this period there were numerous community and church choral groups clamoring for new music to perform. Many of them approached Warren, asking her to write works for them. Thus, a great number of her early choral pieces are written for and dedicated to well-known choral organizations in various parts of the nation.

During one year alone - 1922, her earliest as a published choral composer - four of her sacred choruses went into print: *Arise My Heart and Sing!*, *Christmas Morn*, *Christ Went Up Into the Hills*, and *From Glory Unto Glory*. The same year also saw publication of two of her secular choral works, *Fairy Hills of Dream* and *Flower Chorus in Spring*. Since that time she has written more than ninety compositions for mixed chorus, women's, and men's choruses, *a cappella*, or with organ, piano or orchestra, and today continues writing in this genre.

Besides creative stimulation, New York offered other pleasures for a pretty young woman. Elinor's friend

Mildred Wohlford was now studying at Columbia, where
her roommate was an aspiring young actress, Helen
Gahagan. Later a renowned political figure, following
marriage to actor Melvyn Douglas, Helen first established
herself as an actress, writer and singer. At the *thé
dansants* given at Columbia, Elinor found the young
actress to be the most glamorous person she had ever
seen. Theatrical and romantic-looking, Helen Gahagan
would sweep into the room, wearing an ultra-sophisticated
hat, riveting all eyes upon her. Through these two friends
the young composer met a number of college men, who
took her to dances at West Point, Princeton and Cornell.
Dinner and theatre invitations and parties at college
fraternities provided the composer's only other departures
from her intense musical studies. Mildred Wohlford recalls
that though Elinor dressed simply and looked younger than
the rest of their friends, she was very pretty, with an
appealing charm that made her popular with the more
sophisticated college men. Elinor had a great talent for
mimicry - she could imitate any stage personality with
uncanny accuracy. When her friends got together to play
charades, she was always in demand because of this talent.

She was careful, at these gatherings, not to talk
about her career. Anxious to fit in and not to be thought
"different," the young composer, when her dates asked
what she was doing in New York, would casually mention
she was studying music and enjoying being in the big city,
avoiding reference to the impressive reputation she had
already begun to achieve.

Through her work with Frank LaForge, Warren met some of the greatest concert and opera singers of the day, many of whom coached with LaForge, renowned as the most celebrated vocal coach and accompanist of his time. He advised accompanists on tour to memorize their accompaniments, which would enable them to watch the singer at all times. Should the singer falter or "need a little help," as he diplomatically phrased it, the accompanist - thoroughly familiar with the material - could provide essential support to get him or her back on track. LaForge also counseled singers on the importance of forming the consonants properly. It is easy to sing the vowels, said he, but necessary also to learn the technique of proper consonant formation.

At her lessons, Warren would study and play examples from the great song literature, after which LaForge would discuss their tradition, poetic background, and points of expression and interpretation. Finally, he would have her play them for a singer. In this way, she became thoroughly familiar with the extensive classical repertoire - the great German *lieder* and the French musical literature, as well as contemporary art songs.

LaForge impressed upon his students that the accompanist was not a subordinate but an ensemble player; an integral part of any song. Elinor Warren thoroughly absorbed this idea. Her songs are distinguished for the pianistic quality of their accompaniments and the way in which piano and vocal lines meld to express the spirit of the work as a whole. Though these accompaniments are frequently virtuosic - the creation of a composer who is also a concert pianist - they are saved from overwhelming the singer by Warren's reverence for text, as well as her consideration of the voice. The composer believes that the music she writes must first of all serve the poet's intent and the emotions expressed and then carry the interpretation beyond words. Many singers speak of their pleasure in her vocal lines. One soprano claims she learned breath control singing Warren's long phrases; other singers comment on how well the music lies in the voice and how intelligently the words are used. Sylvia Lee, Metropolitan Opera coach and teacher of vocal interpretation at Philadelphia's Curtis Institute, believes all singers "interested in the life of their throats" should sing Warren songs, because she is one of the few contemporary composers who write "new thoughts that are both singable and listenable."

In addition to work in his studio, Warren was invited by Frank LaForge to appear in programs he arranged at Fordham University. On these programs she would usually play a group of solos, then would accompany her teacher's advanced students, who were preparing for their concert debuts.

The composer frequently brought new songs to her lessons for LaForge's critique. Himself a renowned composer of art songs, LaForge offered suggestions that often proved enlightening and helpful. To him, she dedicated her song, *The Touch of Spring.*

After several months of work together, LaForge urged his student to consider undertaking a new career: accompanist for Metropolitan Opera stars on their national tours. America had entered the era when such tours were much in demand; the greatest singers and instrumentalists were taking to the road, bringing their art not only to the large cities, but to small towns throughout America and abroad.

Exhilarated at the prospect of working with great singers, Warren realized she would learn much from these associations to help her as a composer. As she was to say later, "I cannot think of a more valuable project for a composer of art songs than to experience an extended period of accompanying a singer ... frequently, the more important lessons are 'caught and not always taught.'"

A word from LaForge was sufficient and soon Elinor had entered the world of "the little black dress," as one of her friends, also an accompanist, put it. Female accompanists, especially ones as attractive as Warren, were expected to play down their appearance onstage, so as not to divert attention from the main attraction, the singer. Lucrezia Bori went so far as to have her secretary write in advance to her accompanists, suggesting that "a little black dress" would be most appropriate. In this instance, not wanting to be put down and not yet knowing Bori, Elinor bought the smartest black silk dress she could find; it was trimmed with glimpses of pink. When the astonished Bori first set eyes on her chic accompanist, she exclaimed with a laugh, "Is *that* your little black dress?"

Being a composer with a growing reputation, Warren merited more than just the title of "accompanist." Concert programs listed her as "assisting artist" and she was given part of the program for a group or two of piano solos, as well as accompanying the singer, who always included some of her songs on the program.

LaForge, understanding the sensitivities of his young student, cautioned her against touring with certain stars whose temperaments he knew to be difficult. But he suggested her to Metropolitan Opera soprano star Florence Easton, who became the first concert artist with whom Elinor toured. Their collaboration continued for four years; their friendship, as long as Easton lived. It is to Easton that the composer dedicated one of her most enduring songs, *Lady Lo-Fu*.

Before joining the Metropolitan, Florence Easton had been a leading singer at the Berlin Opera, and was celebrated, as well, for her concert appearances in Europe. The singer had recently lost her only daughter, a girl about Warren's age, and she lavished a mother's affection upon her new accompanist. Warren lived some of the time at the soprano's Long Island home and some of the time at the Algonquin Hotel, near the singer's suite, while they worked together preparing the three different programs they would take on their national tours each season.

Joking she was maladept at page-turning, Warren took her mentor LaForge's advice and memorized all her accompaniments for these tours.

It was at this time that a renowned opera star concocted a small fabrication which was to plague the composer for many years. Though now twenty-two, Elinor looked much younger. Prior to a tour where she was to play for Margaret Matzenauer, the celebrated diva decid-

ed to eliminate five or six years from her accompanist's
real age so that she could be introduced in interviews as
the contralto's young protegè. Elinor *was* young, but
billing her as a "teen-age" prodigy seemed to Matzenauer
and her concert manager a desirable publicity extra.
Embarrassed, but unable to stop the snowballing
fabrication, the young woman said nothing as she saw her
incorrect age appear in numerous biographical references.
Many of these publications have perpetuated the inaccuracies to this day.

The basically reclusive composer found herself looking
forward to new places and audiences on tour. Onstage she
would alleviate stage fright during her piano solo groups
by concentrating on the privilege she was being given to
offer wonderful music to audiences. For Easton she played
the great German *lieder*, the French song literature, and
many of the major soprano arias, as well as a closing
group of her own songs. More importantly, she learned
about singing; how the meaning of the words should be
made plain to an audience, what the voice - even a great
voice - is and is not capable of doing.

Besides Easton, two other singers with whom she first
worked during this period were to profoundly affect her
life and career: Lawrence Tibbett and Richard Crooks.

Though Elinor's father was not actively involved with
the choir at the regular services in his church, he maintained a continuing interest in the group's development.
James Warren was particularly impressed with a young
baritone soloist who had his first choir job at Warren's
church. His name was Lawrence Tibbett.

Tibbett, born in Bakersfield, California, was already
married and the father of twins as he tried to launch a
successful singing career in Los Angeles. The interest,
advice and guidance given him by James Warren remained
close to the singer's heart throughout his life. When
visiting Los Angeles, Tibbett always came to see Warren,
whom he called "Uncle Jim." His love of this family is
apparent in the telegram he sent the Warrens on their
golden wedding anniversary in 1945. Away on tour, he
could not be present, but he said:

Dear Aunt Maude & Uncle Jim:

How happy it would have made me could I have been with you on this great occasion in your rich and generous lives. Nothing would have thrilled me so much as to have been able to be present and to have expressed in song the love and gratitude which I feel for you. Though Jane and I are thousands of miles away, yet we are with you in thought and spirit, celebrating this really golden day.

With loving affection,
Lawrence Tibbett

When gone from the Metropolitan Opera on his long concert tours, Tibbett delighted in introducing to his audiences numerous Elinor Remick Warren songs, among them *Wander Shoes, Lonely Roads, My Parting Gift, Golden Yesterdays*, and her setting of the unusual and distinctive D.H. Lawrence poem, *Piano*. For some of his Western concerts, Warren would appear with him as accompanist and assisting artist. The composer remembers that one of Tibbett's greatest gifts was an ability to make each song he sang a miniature drama. As they worked together in rehearsal, she would be aware that his chief concern lay not just with vocal production but also with interpretation. She recalls the poignancy of his singing and the particular beauty he would bring to the more delicate and fragile art songs, as well as the vigor and power he could command when a song required it.

Though Tibbett proved significant to her career, no other musical artist exerted a greater influence, both personally and professionally, than the singer whom many consider the greatest tenor America has produced, Richard Crooks.

Born in Trenton, New Jersey, Crooks began appearing on the concert stage at the age of twelve. After serving in World War I, he established his reputation as a great recitalist and made successful appearances with the New York Symphony. Later, he appeared in opera in Hamburg and Berlin, and in 1933, made his much-heralded debut with the Metropolitan Opera, where he appeared for the next ten years.

Warren and Crooks met under hilarious circumstances when she was engaged to accompany him in joint recital with Easton in Louisville, Kentucky. The night had turned cold and stormy. As Warren began the very soft introductory phrases of Crooks's first song, Schubert's *Du Bist Die Ruh*, hailstones rained down upon the auditorium's tin roof, just above the stage. Warren found herself in the horrifying predicament of being unable to hear a sound from Crooks; she had to interpret the tenor's lip movements in order to keep the accompaniment with him. Out of this unusual beginning developed a firm friendship with Crooks and his wife Mildred, a friendship so close that years later, long after the singer had ended his career, he came out of retirement just once: to sing Warren's new song, *For You With Love*, at her daughter's wedding.

Crooks introduced many Warren songs on his long concert tours throughout the United States and abroad, among them *Christmas Candle*, *White Horses of the Sea*, *King Arthur's Farewell*, *Sailing Homeward*, and *Through My Open Window*, the words of the latter written by Mildred Crooks. Moreover, he sang these and others repeatedly on leading national radio broadcasts, bringing them to an even wider audience. But Mildred Crooks recalls that her husband, when he would travel to smaller towns, sometimes had trouble with pianists who would be required to play, on short notice, the difficult Warren accompaniments, which demanded first-class ability. Crooks believed Elinor to be an exceptionally gifted pianist and thought she could have had a brilliant concert career had she not eventually chosen composition over performing. He enjoyed the times she played for him in recital. When the tours extended to more than one day, Mildred would join them.

While living in the East, Warren spent memorable weekends with the Crooks at their New York apartment and at their house in nearby Seagirt, New Jersey. But, though she played occasional concerts with both Crooks and Tibbett, as well as with Margaret Matzenauer and Grete Stueckgold, another leading Metropolitan Opera star, her time for touring in that early period of her career was largely filled by the concerts with Florence Easton.

In 1923, in New York, Warren was engaged by Okeh
Records to make a piano recording. She chose two of the
short concert pieces she often performed on tour:
Papillons by Ole Olsen, and Beethoven's *Country Dance
No. 1.* The company sold over 2,000 copies of the disc in
its first three months of release, and Warren was immed-
iately signed by Okeh for a series of piano recordings.
She made this series in 1925, playing eight more of the
short concert pieces from her repertoire; virtuoso works
by composers such as Schumann, Rachmaninoff and
Moszkowski, as well as one of her own compositions,
Frolic of the Elves.

The young musician would return to Los Angeles each
summer. During the summer season of 1923, she was
engaged to appear with the Los Angeles Philharmonic at
Hollywood Bowl as soloist in Mozart's Concerto in D
Minor. The conductor for this occasion was the well-
known founder-conductor of the Minneapolis Symphony,
Emil Oberhoffer. Oberhoffer had been engaged to conduct
the 1923 season of Bowl concerts. That same season saw
the young Lawrence Tibbett make his first appearance
before a large audience in his Hollywood Bowl debut.

Warren recalls Oberhoffer's graciousness to her. At
rehearsal, after she had finished playing the concerto, he
addressed the orchestra members: "This, gentlemen, is how
Mozart should be played - by a lovely young woman,
filled with the joy of living."

On another of her summer visits home, Elinor began
dating a Los Angeles physician, Raymond Huntsberger, who
was becoming a prominent doctor in the city and whose
sister she had known for many years. Huntsberger,
charming and attractive, was a persistent suitor.
Regardless of a burgeoning career and the experiences of
touring and living in New York, Elinor had led an
extremely sheltered personal life. All the inner feelings
she had never experienced, but could only imagine, she
had put into her music. Looking back, she believes at the
time she agreed to be Huntsberger's bride she was
probably more "in love with love" than with the person.
In 1925, the couple was married in a church wedding at
which Lawrence Tibbett sang songs written by the bride
and by her teacher, Frank LaForge. The newlyweds went

to live in a Tudor-style house on Arden Boulevard in
Hancock Park built for them by her father, just as Maude
Warren's father had built a home for Elinor's parents.

The year following her marriage Elinor was again
invited to be piano soloist with the Los Angeles Philharmonic, this time during its regular subscription series at
Philharmonic Auditorium. Once more she played the
Mozart Concerto in D Minor, with which she had had
great success three years before at Hollywood Bowl. The
conductor for this performance was the orchestra's
regular maestro, Walter Henry Rothwell. Reviews were
enthusiastic, one critic finding Warren's Mozart to be
"among the loveliest ... I can remember..., true to style,
technically, of admirable poise, graceful in tone."

Raymond and Elinor became the parents of a son,
James, in 1928. However, there had been problems in the
marriage from its start; Elinor realized she could never
have a happy life with Huntsberger. A year after her
son's birth she began divorce proceedings.

With her baby, the composer now lived alone in her
Arden Boulevard house, during which time she studied
piano with the renowned Italian pianist-composer Paolo
Gallico and appeared in recitals at nearby cities.

In the late twenties and during the 1930's, the
Community Concerts Corporation, founded by seven important New York impresarios, was making the concert tour
big business throughout America. Singers traveled the
nation presenting not only the music of established composers of the past, but of new American composers as
well. Chief among the latter was Warren, whose songs,
though stylistically akin to French Impressionism, bore an
open, frank clarity that was distinctly American. She was
becoming known abroad, also, as American concert artists
of international stature carried her songs with them on
tours throughout the world.

During this period, she would be gone from home for
several weeks at a time, leaving her young son with her
parents, while she toured through the Western states with
contralto Margaret Matzenauer and soprano Grete
Stueckgold. These Metropolitan stars, too, always included
on their programs a group of her songs, Matzenauer scor-

ing a great success with *The Heart of a Rose*, which she later included in a published volume of favorite art songs from her repertoire.

Warren had touched upon the study of orchestration as far back as her years with Gertrude Ross and later worked in this genre with Clarence Dickinson, though he had given her more study of counterpoint and form than of orchestration. During the period she was living alone, Warren felt the need to learn even more about the orchestra, and to follow new roads in writing for it. Her first teacher, Kathryn Cocke, who had entrèe to most of the great instrumentalists appearing in Los Angeles on their national tours, brought the celebrated composer-violinist-conductor, Georges Enesco, to Elinor's house to meet the young composer and hear some of her songs. Enesco, whom Warren remembers as being a short, stocky, and pleasant man who spoke English fluently, listened to the music with enthusiasm and interest. From him, Warren first heard about Nadia Boulanger, who had already become mentor to so many American composers of the era. Enesco suggested it would be a great opportunity if Elinor could go to Paris to study with Boulanger. Warren already had in mind the idea for a large work based on Tennyson's *Idylls of the King*. Enesco advised her that a period of study with Boulanger would help greatly with launching the new project. But she demurred, explaining that she was undergoing a difficult period of adjustment and had a young child whose needs must be considered. At this the older man smiled: "There are babies in France, too, you know."

However, her parents' complete lack of interest in the idea of their daughter's going to Paris to study caused Warren to put aside all thoughts of such a drastic move. She did, however, seriously pursue the study of orchestration and for the ensuing two years worked intensively with Allard de Ridder, principal violist of the Los Angeles Philharmonic. When he left to become conductor of the Vancouver Symphony, she continued on her own, analyzing scores and studying books on the form and techniques of orchestration by great pedagogues and composers. One, by Rimsky-Korsakov, she found indispensable; she uses it today as an occasional reference.

Warren's eldest son, Jim, has vivid memories of his mother during the years they lived alone in the house on Arden Boulevard. He recalls being cautioned never to bother her when she was working, but at 11:30 every morning she would come out to the backyard where he played and would talk and play with him before going back into the house to begin work again. He loved to stand by the steps and watch her at the piano, though at first he did not know she was a composer as well as a pianist. He assumed all children had mothers who played music. His mother would occasionally give parties at home and have friends to visit, among them many of the musicians with whom she was associated. Once, he recalls, Grete Stueckgold was working on repertoire at the house with his mother and took time out to clown about with him, playing a kazoo she fashioned out of a comb.

Warren's first major work with orchestra was *The Harp Weaver*, set to a narrative poem by Edna St. Vincent Millay, *The Ballad of the Harp Weaver*, which had won the Pulitzer Prize in 1922. Millay had been reluctant to let her poems be set to music, feeling the works to be complete in themselves. After one of the poet's readings in Los Angeles during the winter of 1930, Elinor Warren was introduced to her by mutual friends. Bringing up the issue of permission, the composer said she had several times been forced to abandon the idea of setting Millay poems, because of the poet's policy of requiring the full music manuscript to be submitted before permission could be granted. Surprisingly, Millay said she had changed her policy and Warren had her permission to use any of her poems; moreover, it would please her.

Warren considers *The Harp Weaver* to be a modern-day miracle play. Clarence Dickinson's wife, Helen, had introduced her to the poem, based on an ancient Irish myth, during the composer's student days in New York. As she began to work with the idea, she became convinced that it needed the breadth which many voices could provide. Thus she decided to set it for women's chorus with baritone soloist.

But when the work was nearing completion, a letter from Millay's agent at Brandt and Brandt proved unnerving. Millay had ordered that there were to be no repetitions of words or phrases. In a letter to the agent, Warren offered her rebuttal: in music, for correct balance and musical emphasis, a word must often be repeated. Seeking ammunition, she had carefully studied the score for Deems Taylor's opera, *The King's Henchman*, for which Millay had written the libretto, comparing it with the text of the published book. She noted many instances of words and whole phrases being repeated, adding that she had set poems by Noyes, Masefield, Hodgson and Carman, among many others. In no instance had there been concern from these poets about entrusting her with their poems.

These arguments, plus Millay's words to her at their meeting, overcame all objections. In fact, the composer was granted permission to change the work's title to *The Harp Weaver* from the longer and original title, and later, in another work, *Sonnets for Soprano and String Quartet*, to alter a word of the Millay text which Warren found to be unsingable.

Millay's ambivalence when approached about having a poem set to music is not typical of most of the poets Warren has encountered. In fact, throughout her career she has been deluged with poems from unknown poets who hoped to have their words set to music. Of the stellar poets she has contacted, most have been pleased, though some have made exorbitant financial demands, such as a relatively large advance fee and fifty percent of all royalties from sales of the resultant song. However, the poet A.A. Milne, writing in his miniature hand from London, denied Warren permission to set any of the poems from *When We Were Very Young*. He preferred that one composer have the exclusive right to set all his poetry, and the one he had chosen earlier composed music which, he wrote, "has proved extremely popular."

On the other hand when, in 1932, Warren wrote Robert Frost requesting permission to set his poem *Stopping by Woods on a Snowy Evening*, he responded in a handwritten note from Amherst, Massachusetts:

My Dear Miss Warren:
   I shall of course be pleased to have you
set *Stopping by Woods* to music. You must be
sure to let me have it when you do. I am
trying to imagine how you will make it
sound.
   My thanks for having liked it ...

Unfortunately, the press of other projects intervened
and Warren never set the lovely Frost classic, though she
has since included another Frost work in one of her com-
positions-in-progress.

From her earliest childhood, when attending orchestra
concerts, Elinor was inclined to single out the harp as a
focus for musical attention. While still in high school, she
began study of the harp, eventually playing well enough
that in local recitals she would sometimes present one
group of accompaniments on the instrument. Though this
novelty proved attractive to audiences, she soon realized
she could not manage enough hours for both harp and
piano practice, along with her main occupation, composing.
Finally, she abandoned the harp after several years of
study and performance with it. However, she makes extensive use of the instrument in many of her orchestrations.

The Harp Weaver is the most personal of all the composer's works. A fantasy about a boy and his mother in
lonely circumstances, it parallels her own life at the time,
as she struggled to raise her young son by herself. Though
the poem tells of a mother giving her life for the welfare
of her boy, at a deeper level it symbolizes the gift of
life from parent to child, from God to man.

Though it is a major work, *The Harp Weaver* reflects
the poignancy and intimacy of Elinor Warren's songs.
Words and music are closely melded and mirror the
mother's weaving - the focus of Millay's poem. In the
work's orchestration, the harp is featured but does not
predominate; in the piano-vocal version it is offered as an
optional solo instrument through one appropriate section -
and in that version the work is most often heard.

The baritone soloist represents the boy grown into
manhood, recalling events from his youth. The women's
chorus tells the story further, representing the boy him-

self when events of the story occur. At first the two are separated, but as the composition progresses the boy's thoughts are joined musically to the man's remembering, clearly underscoring the story's timelessness and its spiritually triumphant conclusion.

A piano-vocal score was published in 1932. In its orchestral version, the work was first performed, circa 1935, by the leading Los Angeles choral group of the time, John Smallman's Cecilian Singers, at the city's principal concert hall, Philharmonic Auditorium. It received acclaim from audience and press alike, the *Los Angeles Times* noting Warren "has caught the stark and haunting beauty of the Millay poem in amazing fashion in the rich instrumentation."

A New York premiere was also important for the young composer; that took place in April of 1936, at Carnegie Hall, Antonia Brico conducting the New York Women's Symphony Orchestra, the Treble Clef Chorus of the White Plains Contemporary Club, and Raoul Nadeau, baritone soloist. *New York Times* music critic Olin Downes called the work "charming music, characterized by real feeling and by a very sympathetic treatment of the text ..." He went on to note, however, that "in places ... the expression comes perilously near the sentimental. But we would that more American composers were less afraid to be sentimental and that they possessed the genuine creative talent that is Miss Warren's." Composer Deems Taylor, writing for the *New York Evening World*, observed that Warren "has ideas, and an undeniable gift for music writing."

The work soon had numerous performances, among them one at the 1939 San Francisco Exposition, which was repeated at the San Francisco Opera House. *The Harp Weaver* has proven to be among Warren's most enduring and best-loved works, both in this country and abroad. Among its later performances was one at Siena, Italy, in 1969, when Wilfrid Pelletier presented the piano-harp version in concert. Upon that occasion, the conductor wrote Warren, "... the reception by the public was very rewarding. It is a beautiful work, the music so inspired. I really thank you with all my heart to have had this opportunity to present your work in Siena."

4. Z. WAYNE GRIFFITH

While Warren was at work on the orchestration of *The Harp Weaver*, Richard Crooks, on a long nationwide tour, introduced in Los Angeles a new song, then still in manuscript, which she had written for him, *White Horses of the Sea*. Warren attended his recital. When it came time for the new song to be performed, Crooks announced from the stage that its composer was in the audience; he asked her to come up and play it for him, which she did.

In the audience that night was an aspiring young tenor named Zachary Wayne Griffin, who already knew some of the Warren songs. Wayne Griffin later declared that when the youthful composer came onstage and proceeded to "tear into the rousing, difficult accompaniment," for him "all the bells started ringing, then and there!"

Griffin's widowed mother had brought Wayne, his brother, and his sister to Los Angeles from Kentucky when they were children. At the age of eleven, he had played the Orpheum Circuit for one season, where he was billed as a boy soprano soloist. Later, as a student at Oregon State, he managed to hold down seven jobs off-campus, at the same time he was establishing a Western division record in sprinting.

At the time he first saw Elinor Warren on a concert stage, Griffin was studying voice with hopes of a serious career as a singer. Elinor, a friend of his singing teacher, was later introduced to him at a small party in the teacher's home. The couple started seeing each other and soon fell in love. However, they were to wait several years before marrying. Griffin had accepted a position in San Francisco with the NBC radio network and felt he must prove himself in the new career before taking on the responsibilities of a wife and family. Radio was at its height in popularity; at first, Griffin gained experience as a writer, eventually becoming a leading producer of popular shows, among them *The Maxwell House Hour* and the DuPont *Cavalcade of America*. Never far from the music scene, while at NBC he was also writing music reviews for the San Francisco newspapers.

During Griffin's years in San Francisco, Elinor again faced lonely times, though the two wrote to each other every day and her fiancé drove down to Los Angeles whenever possible to see her on weekends. Meanwhile, she filled her time with composing and with occasional concerts in nearby cities, sometimes accompanying Crooks or Tibbett when they were appearing on the West Coast.

During this period she left her home and child for only one extended tour of the West, with Spanish soprano Lucrezia Bori. She had been recommended to Bori by Frank LaForge, and this was to be a particularly important occasion: the Metropolitan Opera star's farewell concert tour. Bori had surprised friends and colleagues by announcing her plan to retire at the summit of her career. As she wrote Warren: "I am so happy to have the courage, before the physical disabilities arrive, to quit - but still a little sad." As always, on this tour Elinor played one or sometimes two groups of piano solos and accompanied Bori, who included on her programs Warren's song, *The Little Betrothed*, which had been dedicated to her.

Though some contemporaries have commented on Bori's cool, somewhat remote personality, Warren remembers her as being unfailingly gracious and considerate. While undergoing the rigors of an extended tour, she always found time to listen to the many young singers who sought her advice. One singer who never forgot her kindness to him was Richard Crooks who, in 1933, made his Metropolitan Opera debut singing Des Grieux to Bori's Manon in the Massenet opera. He later told Warren that the soprano had gone out of her way to be helpful and to put him at ease for this important performance. Similarly, when she was in Los Angeles preparing for her tour with Warren, she wrote her young accompanist: "From 9:30 to eleven I will receive all of them [the press] ... I will love to give you a little publicity in your own town. Please do come to the Hotel in the morning." That tour began a friendship with the great diva which lasted until her death in 1960.

In 1933, Arnold Schoenberg settled in the United States. By 1934, he had arrived in Los Angeles and the following year began teaching at the University of Southern California. Before the invitation arrived from USC, the eminent Austrian composer taught students privately. Julia Howell and Pauline Alderman, faculty members at the USC School of Music, invited a select group of musicians and composers - among them the 23-year-old John Cage and Elinor Warren - to attend a series of weekly lectures given by the composer throughout the spring of 1935 at his Hollywood residence. Warren remembers Schoenberg as being a small man with olive skin. During his lectures, he talked primarily about his own works and techniques, spending several weeks analyzing his *Third String Quartet*, which had been composed in 1927. Once, discussing a composition he was then writing, Schoenberg noted there were 1,004 measures of it, and he pointed out the theme - "at least I *think* it is the theme." Though acknowledging Schoenberg to be a towering influence on 20th century music, Warren feels she gained little from his lectures; his twelve-tone techniques held scant relationship to her choice of musical expression and to her work.

Finally, after four years in San Francisco, Wayne Griffin had an opportunity to return to Los Angeles as head of radio production for the CBS Western outlet, KHJ, which was later followed by an appointment to head the radio department of BBDO. His major assignment there was to produce the *Burns and Allen* radio show, starring George Burns and Gracie Allen, which, under his aegis, became one of the most popular programs in broadcast history. By now, Griffin had given up all idea of a career as a concert singer, because of allergies and many bouts of asthma which would have limited him professionally. Still, he remained a fine tenor and, following their marriage, enjoyed performing his wife's songs with her for informal recital programs.

Local newspapers and music publications duly recorded the marriage of Elinor Remick Warren and Z. Wayne Griffin, which took place shortly before Christmas, December 12, 1936, in the St. Francis Chapel of the Mission Inn at Riverside, then a favored place for

Southern California weddings. Only immediate family and
close friends were present. Ringbearer was the composer's
young son Jim, whose name was later legally changed to
Griffin.

Following a short honeymoon, the couple returned to
the bride's house, where they were to live for the next
two years, until a growing family forced them to seek
larger quarters.

For Elinor's wedding present, Lucrezia Bori had
searched the London antique shops to find something representative of her composer-friend's career. It turned out
to be a pair of candelabra ornamented with silver-winged
horses. The singer wrote that to her they represented the
song *White Horses of the Sea* which, though not for her
voice, she felt to be one of Warren's finest songs.
Moreover, that song had marked an important moment for
its composer, since Richard Crooks had sung it the first
time Griffin saw his bride-to-be. These same candelabra,
lighted each evening, still grace the composer's dining
room.

The late Betty Haldeman, whose friendship with Elinor
was close over many years and who also shared the composer's musical interests, believed marriage to Wayne
Griffin opened up life a great deal for her friend. In a
conversation prior to her death, she recalled, "Before
Elinor knew Wayne, she was living for her music, concentrating almost solely on her work. Wayne introduced her
to a new group of friends, new areas of life, different
and broader interests. He made life more well-rounded for
her."

Throughout a long and devoted marriage, Elinor and
Wayne Griffin were to lead very separate and independent
careers - both in the public eye, both very successful.
However, this was never to detract from the exceptional
closeness of their marriage and family life; each would
always support the other in career affairs as well as at
home.

5. CAREER AND FAMILY

During the 1930's, heyday of the art song in America, Warren songs were being heard throughout the world. Lawrence Tibbett programmed them on his various concert tours and on radio as well. Sometimes the composer would receive word from the singer about these radio appearances. "Try to listen in tonight. Singing *Sweetgrass Range*. Affectionately, Lawrence" came a telegram in 1936. That year, in her Town Hall recital, Grete Stueckgold sang a group of five Warren songs, prompting a New York critic to write: "The songs were eminently worth while musically, well made and of strong characterization."

Elinor's friend from her New York days, Helen Gahagan, who had become Mrs. Melvyn Douglas, joined the concert circuit and, toward the end of the 1930's, programmed the composer's *White Horses of the Sea*, which she sang with orchestra. On several tours, reaching as far as Australia, Richard Crooks programmed Warren songs, as did Tibbett, John Charles Thomas, Rose Bampton, Kirsten Flagstad, Gladys Swarthout, Marjorie Lawrence, Lauritz Melchior, Nadine Conner, Nelson Eddy, Jessica Dragonette, and Jeanette MacDonald. In succeeding years, the roster of celebrated singers performing Warren songs in concert or on radio would grow to include, as well, Helen Traubel, Risë Stevens, Bidu Sayao, Dorothy Maynor, Dorothy Kirsten, Blanche Thebom, Eleanor Steber, Eileen Farrell, Regina Resnik, and from the Broadway musical stage, John Raitt. Always, a new Warren song found ready acceptance among America's and Europe's leading artists.

In 1937, Nelson Eddy sang Warren's *My Parting Gift* at a Los Angeles appearance. Believing he had not done justice to the song, he wrote the composer a letter of apology: "After doing so poorly with your song I felt ashamed to face you. I think I can get hold of it eventually and make it go. Coming at the end of the program it was a slight strain on the limited larynx. I believe it is more of a mental hazard, however, and hope to lick it." This was typical, says Warren, of the singer's overly modest evaluation of his vocal abilities. She remembers Nelson Eddy, who, with his wife Ann, was a close friend, as being a very sensitive person, perfectionistic and always too critical of his musical gifts. She greatly admired his rich baritone and enjoyed evenings where the two of them - their spouses an attentive audience - would pour through entire books of Brahms or Schumann *lieder*.

Upon her arrival in America, the celebrated Norwegian soprano Kirsten Flagstad began including Warren songs in her concert programs; at her Carnegie Hall debut recital, December 11, 1935, she featured the composer's *White Horses of the Sea*. The Warren songs had been introduced to the singer by her accompanist, Edwin McArthur. Until her retirement in 1953, Flagstad programmed the composer's works in her concert appearances worldwide.

Joining the Metropolitan Opera in 1935, after a season at Bayreuth, Flagstad was acclaimed as the greatest living Wagnerian soprano, and similarly celebrated as a concert singer. So extraordinary were her vocal powers, she could be equally at home in Warren's sweeping *White Horses of the Sea* and the dramatic *We Two*, or in the delicate *Snow Towards Evening* or *Christmas Candle*. Other Warren songs Flagstad enjoyed privately. In 1947, she wrote the composer about the song *Come Away*, which she loved singing at home in Norway during the war; however, feeling it was not for her voice, she had reluctantly decided not to venture it in public. Flagstad often closed her programs with Warren songs; reviewers commented that they could have been written for her, so well did they suit her voice and temperament. In Denver, according to one critic, the climax of *White Horses of the Sea*, "...practically had the audience out of its seats."

Though new compositions continued to flow from her pen during the 1930's, Warren did not neglect her career as solo pianist and accompanist, appearing locally in recital and continuing to tour with leading singers.

Rare recordings of her concert appearances attest to Warren's exceptional pianistic gifts. But though the

composer admits to having power and a sure technique,
she acknowledges that her small hands, which can barely
reach beyond the octave, have made the performing of
certain concert works virtually impossible. Nonetheless,
critics at her piano recitals have written of her "depth
and a certain grandeur," "poetic refinement," and "chaste-
ness of tone and technique backed by a deep resource of
well-tempered power." One scribe noted gratuitously, "The
artist also gave quite as much satisfaction to the eye as
to the ear."

Though for performing her appearance could be considered an asset, it proved a subtle strike against her as
a composer, as did her sex and the fact that she did not
have to support herself by her music. Later, her husband's
growing prominence in musical and civic affairs also offered a target for persons who would detract from the
composer's obvious ability in her field, even though that
ability had found world recognition long before her marriage to him. Through the years, Warren has been confronted with interviewers seemingly more interested in her
life style and in the problems of being a woman composer
than in her attitudes about the work itself.

During the mid-1930's, the composer recalls being
engaged to record, on 78 RPM, a series of piano accompaniments of art song classics, primarily for use by
teachers and by singers learning repertoire. Though details
of these recordings are missing, Warren remembers that
the discs, which she made in Los Angeles, proved useful
and successful, earning her royalties for a number of
years.

During the early years of her marriage, Warren continued to tour with leading concert artists. But she soon
began to begrudge the time spent away from home. Moreover, her career as a composer was burgeoning. Eventually
she cut down on appearances and, thereafter, seldom was
seen in public as a pianist except to accompany singers in
her songs. However, practice sessions at her piano were
always a part of each day's regimen - as they continue
to be.

This decision to leave the concert field as a performer may have been due in part to something beyond

the desire for more time at home. Elinor believes that for a woman "anything creative is more satisfying than being a performer. It may be slower to accomplish, but it can be done, and done successfully. One can't be truly creative and be a full-time performer. One must be willing to sacrifice 'free time' for one's goals."

Though continuing to write the art songs that had made her reputation, now that she was free to give her undivided musical attention to composing Warren found herself increasingly attracted by the challenge of writing large choral works.

Earlier - by 1935 - the composer had begun work on a project that had been contemplated for some time, one she knew she would spend several years in writing. This composition, *The Passing of King Arthur*, would eventually be regarded among her finest achievements. While still in high school at Westlake, she became intrigued by the Arthurian legends as written by Tennyson in *Idylls of the King*, which was read to her class by Jessica Vance, one of the school's two principals and her English teacher. Even then, Elinor had conceived the idea of one day writing a large composition based on portions of Tennyson's work; at the time Georges Enesco suggested she go to Paris to study with Nadia Boulanger she already had its form in mind.

Noble and fraught with drama, the choral symphony, for mixed chorus and orchestra with tenor and baritone soloists, portrays the death of the legendary English ruler. The composition's original title was later changed by the composer prior to the publication of a later edition and after three major performances; she did not wish to emphasize the death of King Arthur so much as the drama of the story and the developing spiritual qualities of the poem. The edition, published in 1974, was retitled *The Legend of King Arthur*. Three excerpts, the orchestral *Intermezzo*, the *a cappella* chorus *More Things Are Wrought By Prayer*, and the aria *King Arthur's Farewell*, are published separately and frequently performed apart from the work.

Though she made revisions in later years - all included in the last published piano-vocal edition and its orchestral counterpart - the original edition essentially achieves Warren's vision of the work and is faithful to the majesty of the Tennyson text. However, the undertaking of a large and significant composition by a young composer who, though she had written for orchestra, had had scant practical experience in creating such a massive work, represented an act of extraordinary dedication. Though she never altered the essential form of the composition, at one point - dissatisfied with her orchestration - the composer discarded much of it, putting aside the manuscript for many months. After three decades and further performances she was still polishing details of orchestration, at times eliminating the orchestra to emphasize the importance of the words and the soloist's vocal line. "I am obviously a composer who is a 'tinkerer,'" Warren explains.

Tennyson's epic poem on the death of Arthur mirrors Warren's affinity for subjects of spiritual and noble drama. Like the English composers Ralph Vaughan Williams and Frederick Delius and France's Arthur Honegger, the composer strives in much of her work to achieve a sublime sensitivity; a mystical perfection through beauty of sound and the blending of music and text. Nowhere in her music have these qualities been more fully realized than in *The Legend of King Arthur*. Warren remembers the inspiration she experienced throughout the writing of this composition; how she could hardly wait each morning to begin upon it; the excitement she felt about every aspect of the work. A highlight of the choral symphony is the aria *More Things Are Wrought By Prayer*, sung first by the dying king, then repeated by the chorus *a cappella*. Warren recalls that just before she began to write this portion of the composition a favorite cousin died. Deeply moved by the loss of her relative, the composer wove her own feelings about death into the fabric of this profound and touching section.

During the writing of *King Arthur*, Elinor found time to appear on her own weekly radio program about music. Presented for a season of Sunday afternoons during 1938-1939, and heard in the Pacific Coast states over the Mutual-Don Lee Network, the series was written by Warren; it featured her at the piano playing music by the

composers she discussed each week. During every program
Warren offered vignettes and verbal portraits of a great
range of composers from Gluck to Debussy. About the
latter's music she tendered this interesting perception,
which might also be said of her own *Legend of King
Arthur*: "The subjects of Debussy's compositions were
chosen from the external world, but are so full of a
mystic fabric, we feel he looked on the world from some
secluded, distant place." Each program contained approximately three piano compositions, ranging from the well-
known, like the series theme, Schumann's *Dedication*, to
Leschetizky's *Etude Héroïque* or *The Spinning Girls of
Carentec* by Rhené-Baton. Prompted by requests from
listeners, she would occasionally play her own compositions, such as *Frolic of the Elves* - later programmed by
Dame Myra Hess - and *The Fountain*. An entire program
was devoted to a performance of *The Harp Weaver* in its
piano, harp, chorus and baritone solo version.

Though the programs found a large listening audience
that sent in cards and letters requesting the composer to
play and discuss their favorites each Sunday, Warren
announced on March 5 that she was leaving the air for a
concert tour of the West Coast. She promised to return,
but new avenues were opening.

One of these avenues was motherhood. In 1938, a
second son, Z. Wayne, Jr., had been born; soon to come,
in 1940, would be a daughter, Elayne, for whom the
composer wrote her song *To a Blue-Eyed Baby*. Though
friends thought Warren had named Elayne for the fair
heroine of Tennyson's *Idylls of the King*, the name actu-
ally derived from a compound of the Griffins' two given
names: Elinor and Wayne.

In a bantering radio interview four years after her
marriage to Griffin, Elinor said that the secret of success
in marriage was "getting the right husband." When asked
by interviewers which came first - music or motherhood -
she would always respond that her family came ahead of
everything else. However, the added domestic responsibilities did nothing to alter either the quality or the quantity
of her output. She credits this in large measure to an
understanding and helpful husband who, from the outset of
their marriage, tried to shield her from many of the daily

details of living that are wasteful of an artist's creative energy. Moreover, Warren has always been a disciplined, patient and powerfully motivated worker at her craft. Though she complains she works too slowly and often berates herself for not producing more, her catalog consists of nearly two hundred published compositions. All have been written using her maiden name, Elinor Remick Warren. Once, a publisher tried to get away with "E.R. Warren" to obscure her sex. Since then, the composer has steadfastly refused to permit such deception. She now feels, however, that "Remick Warren" might have been a wiser choice. For at the time she gained international recognition, there were still many male musicians who looked askance at a woman composer. Seated beside Eugene Ormandy at a dinner party, Warren found herself on the defensive as the conductor remonstrated with her for not devoting herself completely to "woman's unique responsibility" - raising a large family.

After temporarily setting aside her work on *The Legend of King Arthur*, Elinor wrote other compositions for orchestra, among them *The Fountain* and *Scherzo* - both adapted from solos originally composed for piano - in order to gain the facility she desired before returning to the main task at hand.

The Fountain, a short, impressionistic composition making ample use in its orchestration of the harp Warren loves so well, was inspired by an image the composer had in mind as she began to write it: a peacock comes to bathe in the splashing water of a fountain, as lovers stroll by and drop a coin for luck; the garden is quiet with moonlight, and the fountain sings. "The orchestral colors used are soft, poetic, refined and imaginative," wrote one reviewer.

Back at work on *King Arthur*, Warren spent much of the next three years perfecting the original sketches she had made in 1935-36. By 1940, the composition had been completed. A piano-vocal edition was published and the orchestration placed in its publisher's rental library.

The choral symphony, one hour in length, was brought to the attention of the management and board of the Los Angeles Philharmonic by the friend and advisor of many

young American singers and composers, Dr. Richard Lert.
Lert had programmed the *Intermezzo* for orchestra from
the larger work in several concerts with the Pasadena
Civic Orchestra, of which he was conductor. Moreover,
Warren had sought occasional technical advice from him
while writing the composition. Lert prepared the Los
Angeles Oratorio Society for the premiere and he and his
wife, novelist Vicki Baum of *Grand Hotel* fame, were present to hear the first performance.

Another musician friend of long-standing, Charles
Wakefield Cadman, was slated to have his *First Symphony*
premiered by the Philharmonic the same month as the
King Arthur premiere. From New York, Cadman wrote to
congratulate his younger colleague, adding some words of
advice:

> My dear, I have been through the MILL
> and I know *what* worry and anxiety and tra-
> vail await EVERY creative artist in the birth
> of a new work ... There will be grief, and
> *lots* of it ... I suppose we BOTH will, in the
> American sense and scene, feel ... *JITTERY*,
> and that is a good thing. For any composer
> to feel *SURE* of every passage, to feel sure
> he *CAN'T* go wrong, is to stop all growth
> and expansion creatively. I have felt always
> that YOU were not that type. I have tried
> to be the *same* way. GOD knows, after I do
> a thing, how defective it is in places, and
> how much *better* I *could have* done it ... I
> can't think of any larger form thing I have
> done (chamber work or orch. or opera) where
> I wouldn't like *to do it all over* ... I guess
> you have felt that way too ...

Cadman proved correct in assessing Warren's zeal to
perfect her work. However, he was wrong in predicting
how painful the "birth" of this composition would be.
Warren knew it was ready for performance, and she soon
learned that the guest conductor from England, Albert
Coates, was enthusiastic and cooperative. However, an
interview she gave in 1955 mirrors somewhat Cadman's
sentiments on the subject of "birthing" a new composition:
"I often wonder if an audience has any idea of all that

goes into the presentation of a new orchestral work. Between first sketch and first performance lies a sometimes rocky road. Performance is a matter of minutes; I shudder to think of the mountains of time and the oceans of mental and physical energies it represents for the composer. ... The hard fact is that composing is an arduous, endless labor of love which must be done with the dedication and seclusion of a Franciscan monk. ... However, even with the high cost in time, work, and self-abnegation, composers continue to compose because composition is immensely rewarding. Not financially - that is, not for the symphonic or concert composer - but in a much fuller sense. It is a fascinating, absorbing, inescapable, compelling assignment. When a major work of one's own blood, toil and tears comes to life in a first-class orchestra - well, the long road getting it there is forgotten."

A survey of the newspaper reviews for Warren works shows an overwhelming preponderance of favorable and even rave comments, but none have been more unified in their enthusiasm than those that followed the premiere of *The Legend of King Arthur.* One critic recorded the work was ... "So vital, complex and at times so overwhelming a composition, it created a real sensation."

Late that evening, upon returning home following the triumph of the first of two performances, Elinor found awaiting her a further tribute - a telegram sent by her first teacher, Kathryn Montreville Cocke: "Dear Elinor, What I predicted for you when you were a little girl of five years has tonight been successfully fulfilled in the wonderful performance of your greatest composition. My love and admiration for you and your work has grown yearly and I now predict for you the greatest of success in fulfilling that beautiful gift to the world of music for which God has created you. Congratulations to you from your loving teacher ..."

In large measure this evening had also been Kathryn Cocke's triumph.

Several months after the premiere and its press ballyhoo, the composer received an unusual telephone call. It was from the casting agent for billionaire mogul Howard Hughes then a major motion picture producer. Stating that

that Mr. Hughes had seen Miss Warren's picture in the newspapers, the representative suggested Mr. Hughes wished Miss Warren to come to the studio for a screen test; she had a fresh new face for pictures. The composer demurred, stating she had no interest in being in movies; she was content with being a serious composer. That would be all right, she could still write her music, replied the representative. Amused, Elinor said again she was not interested, adding she was older than most starlets. That was okay, too, rejoined the insistent agent, if only Miss Warren looked like her pictures in the newspaper. What finally dissuaded Hughes's representative was learning the composer was then pregnant and her husband was also a producer. "Oh, we've all heard of your husband," said the disappointed man, finally willing, upon hearing Griffin's name, to give up his unsuccessful talent hunt.

Following the *King Arthur* premiere, excerpts from the full work began receiving important performances. During the summer of 1940, Sir John Barbirolli, at Hollywood Bowl, conducted the *Intermezzo*, an interlude that divides the two sections of the work and features a solo bass clarinet. Pierre Monteux conducted it that fall with the San Francisco Symphony and again in February of 1943 on radio, in an NBC Symphony broadcast. A review noted that the excerpt "held the atmosphere of a reverie and is written with feeling for instrumental timbres, making an interesting and useful addition to symphonic literature." In November of 1941, Richard Crooks, appearing with the National Symphony Orchestra in Washington, D.C., sang *King Arthur's Farewell*, two arias from the larger work which the composer combined into one and which was later published in two keys.

Though work on *The Legend of King Arthur* consumed much of her time, just before and during the early years of her marriage to Griffin, Warren composed some of her most successful songs. Tender, introspective, they deal with her favorite themes for this musical medium: the heart and nature's beauty. Among them are *The Nights Remember*, *By a Fireside*, *If You Have Forgotten* - the latter with a poignant text by Sara Teasdale - and *Snow Towards Evening*, considered to be one of the finest art songs written by an American. In the hushed expectancy of its opening chords, the song captures the gray stillness before snow falls, as night looms. In gently descending and ascending chord patterns, blended with a vocal line drifting gently like the snowflakes the poem describes, the composer superbly achieves what she has said she considers to be her ultimate objective in a song: to reach past the mechanics of notes and staves to an understanding beyond even the words themselves.

Kirsten Flagstad frequently programmed *Snow Towards Evening*, often contrasting it with the powerful *White Horses of the Sea*. Also on Flagstad's concert programs during the 1940's were *We Two*, written for Griffin as an anniversary present, and *Christmas Candle*.

The latter had been dedicated to the composer's three children. So popular did it become that on one December evening in 1940, two singers - Richard Crooks and Lawrence Tibbett - featured it on separate national radio broadcasts. It must be listed first among the most-performed of all Warren songs. In addition to the version for solo voice, its publisher later requested from the composer choral arrangements in six different vocal combinations, both *a cappella* and accompanied. The song has been recorded several times by classical singers and once by a pop artist. Warren recalls one holiday season, waiting for a purchase in a Beverly Hills department store, she was surprised to hear over the store's Muzak system Tony Martin's Decca recording of her song. Though Warren never wrote in a light, popular vein, *Christmas Candle* provided her closest brush with "Hit Parade" status.

One of her most cherished memories of *Christmas Candle* is more private. On a visit to Los Angeles during a nationwide concert tour, Kirsten Flagstad, who rarely accepted social invitations, attended a small dinner party which the Griffins had planned in her honor. At the dinner-table that night, Warren was surprised to hear the soprano quietly ask Griffin, "Do you think Elinor would mind if I sing *Christmas Candle* after dinner?" Knowing that celebrated artists rarely perform at a private party, Elinor was particularly honored when later the soprano filled the music room with her "shining, golden voice" - a voice Warren declares to be the finest she has heard. The composer found Flagstad to be possessed of an engaging warmth and personal charm, as well as a sincere manner.

After completing *The Legend of King Arthur*, Warren - still immersed in Tennyson - searched for another of the poet's works to set. She found it in one of his lighter, but still lengthy, poems based on the fairy tale *The Sleeping Beauty*. She set it for four-part chorus, with soprano, baritone, and bass-baritone soloists. Though first writing it with piano accompaniment she completed an orchestration during the ensuing months. It was copyrighted by its publisher, H.W. Gray, in 1951.

The Sleeping Beauty is written in six sections, titled *The Sleeping Palace, The Sleeping Princess, The Prince's Arrival, The Awakening, The King and Lords, The Departure*. In several respects the work proved to be a disappointment for its composer. Though the story is naive, the music is difficult - beyond the abilities of many college choruses. Thus, *The Sleeping Beauty* is most likely to be performed in sections - notably *The Sleeping Princess*.

During the 1940's, radio had become a major entertainment medium with the American public. Wayne Griffin was now producing one of the most popular of the radio series, *The Burns and Allen Show*, starring George Burns and Gracie Allen. When he took the program to New York for several appearances, Elinor accompanied him. Griffin had earlier received a lucrative business opportunity to relocate in Manhattan and the two had given it serious thought. Warren, too, would benefit professionally by such a move. However, both had elderly parents and other close relatives in Los Angeles; their children were happy there. Deciding the personal sacrifice would be too great, they remained in the West. By now they had moved to larger quarters, to accommodate their growing children. The house they chose in the Hancock Park area of Los Angeles is the house where Warren still lives.

There was always a great deal of music-making in the Griffin household. Though Wayne Griffin had been forced to abandon his earlier plans for a professional singing career because of severe allergies, he continued to enjoy singing the classical literature, as well as his wife's songs. At night when her parents were playing and singing in the downstairs music room, the Griffins' young daughter, Elayne, would steal out of bed and sit at the top of the stairs - listening to her parents' musicmaking, as her mother had done before her.

Though Griffin jokingly admonished his children, "If you break a leg, then and only then may you interrupt your mother when she's composing," all three were remarkably considerate of Warren's work hours. However, the composer always broke off mid-morning to share juice and a romp in the garden with those youngsters not yet in school; later their school hours became her best work hours. Their teachers recall Warren as a concerned parent who helped with homework and deeply involved herself in each child's development. Her belief that home and family came first had been, from the start, more than just idle talk. Though in a candid moment she admitted "there have been times when I thought that always the age just ahead for my children would release me for more time with my music," Warren feels her family has been an important factor in her development as a creative artist. "The more completely mature and well-rounded is a person's own development, the more he or she is equipped to express ideas in music that are valid and universal. Being a wife and mother has expanded my interests and experiences immensely beyond what they would otherwise have been, and I feel this has enriched my music, too." However, she also feels a woman who is working seriously at home in a creative profession must allot for herself undisturbed hours; the problem of time is one of the main factors in the scarcity of women composers, she says, "for composition takes more concentrated and uninterrupted time, perhaps, than any of the other arts." Moreover, when embarked upon a project the composer is continually at work - if not always on paper, at least in the mind.

Each of Warren's children reacted differently to her career. Her eldest son, Jim, became alarmed when it was announced that his mother's choral version of *Christmas Candle* would be performed by his junior high chorus in a school assembly. Upon learning she would be present, he told his mother he didn't know why she had to be there - "None of the other mothers come over to hear *their* songs sung." Jim was further mortified when his pretty mother came onstage and the young boys from his gym class began whistling appreciatively. On the other hand, Wayne, Jr., at the age of four, relished introducing his mother to friends and adding, "She's the composer, you know." At an even younger age, he asked his mother whether he might stand on the street corner and hand out cards that would read, "Elinor Remick Warren, Composer." Later, he recalled his total lack of embarrassment about having a well-known parent, "I'm not above basking in reflected glory - no matter whose glory it is."

Daughter Elayne early decided she wasn't going to take up her mother's profession. "I wouldn't want to do that," she announced to the composer. "You work harder than a cleaning lady!" Later she admitted she had distanced herself from her mother's profession, believing she could never be good enough to compete. As a child she announced she would become a singer, "So I can sing Mother's songs." She did perform one of them, singing *Lady Lo-Fu* in a clear, sweet soprano at her Marlborough School Fine Arts Festival.

Warren's children agreed that their mother never talked much to them about her profession; it was Wayne Griffin who told them about Elinor's renown and instilled in them a pride about it.

Kathryn Cocke was engaged to teach music to each of Warren's two sons. Young Wayne excited the family with early promise. The composer held her breath - was there another Mozart in the making? Then Miss Cocke decided to retire. After sixty years spent in Los Angeles, she moved back to her hometown, Somerville, Tennessee. The "promise," it was discovered, had simply been a great teacher's skill and perseverance.

During her student years with Miss Cocke, Elinor had opportunities to play chamber music; she greatly enjoyed the musical give-and-take of ensemble playing. However, the form proved not to be a particular medium of choice for her as a composer. In the latter half of her career she has successfully set some choral works for chamber orchestra, and her *Sonnets for Soprano* is written with an accompaniment for string quartet or chamber orchestra.

But generally she has preferred working with the many colors to be achieved using full orchestra.

Gregor Piatigorsky once asked her to write a work for cello he could perform in recital. When she did not act on his suggestion, he enjoyed teasing her each time they met, saying, "Here is the composer who hates the cello!"

However she has written a small body of works and arrangements for her own instrument, as well as a *Quintet for Woodwinds and Horn* and a composition for viola and piano. The latter was programmed extensively by William Primrose, particularly during the season of 1944, when he and Richard Crooks toured together in joint recital, he playing Warren's *Poem* and Crooks singing *White Horses of the Sea* - both works written by Warren for these artists.

The *Quintet for Woodwinds and Horn*, premiered in 1937, was a departure for Warren. She says of it, "Usually, composers write music just for the joy of composing. They do not necessarily have a program in mind as a pattern for their work. I had long wanted to write something for woodwinds, and this is the result."

Much performed by the distinguished San Francisco Woodwind Quintet, Warren's composition was considered by critics to be "highly original," its composer an "adept writer for instrumental ensemble." Regardless, she has always felt most stimulated when composing in forms that would seem the converse of each other: full orchestra and solo voice with piano.

In creating a song, Warren regards the music as a framework for and expression of the poet's words. Indeed, she will seldom accept praise for any of her songs, preferring instead to compliment the text, which for her represents the essence of the collaboration. She always spends time speaking the poem before starting to put music to it. In that way, she learns where the accents fall and whether there are words not suited to singing. For her song *Lonely Roads*, set to John Masefield's poem *Personal* which begins "Tramping at night in the cold and wet, I passed the lighted inn, ..." she paced up and down the length of her music room to suggest a rhythm appropriate to the words. That, in turn, brought her an opening melody and a tempo she felt to be correct.

"Composing a song," she has said, "is transposing
words into music. However, the song should be *beyond* the
spoken word. Some poets do not like their poems to be
set to music because they think that words alone can ad-
equately express their thoughts. But it seems to me that
music intensifies the words and glorifies them, their
meaning transcending the printed form."

Singers who perform Warren's songs repeatedly comment on their remarkable blend of text and vocal line.
Rose Bampton, who premiered Warren's song cycle,
Singing Earth, and often included the composer's songs in
her recital programs, now teaches them to her students at
Juilliard. She is impressed by Warren's choice of beautiful
poetry which she sets, says Bampton, "with a real feeling
for the words."

When contemplating a new vocal work, the composer
searches for a text that will impress her literary sense;
then words which are "singable;" finally, ideas which can
be clearly expressed in the vocal line. Warren credits
Lawrence Tibbett with sound advice regarding the latter.
Early in her career the baritone cautioned her never to
write a song whose meaning he could not clearly project
to his audience at first hearing. Otherwise, singer and
listener had failed to communicate. Warren never forgot
his admonition; her song *Who Loves the Rain*, for example,
uses for its text a poem which simply paints a brief and
subtle mood:

> Who loves the rain and loves his home,
> And looks on life with quiet eyes,
> Him will I follow through the storm,
> And at his hearthfire keep me warm;
> Nor hell nor heav'n shall that soul surprise -
> Who loves the rain and loves his home,
> And looks on life with quiet eyes.

Clearly evident in Warren's songs is the composer
seeking her inspiration from the words; rhythm and textual
sense shaping the music. Warren contends that the composer, more than other creative artists, must work through
instinct and feeling. She believes her compositions have

sprung not so much from personal experience as from a vivid imagination. "I cannot tell you what gives me the idea for a composition. It might be a poem, or just the germ of an idea from somewhere, or an expression in music of a mood or emotion. I first work out a plan away from the piano, and as I get into it, it multiplies and compounds." Only when its general structure is formed in her mind does she then begin working at the piano.

As do most composers, Warren sometimes reworks earlier material from a new viewpoint. But record producer Lance Bowling, who has recorded the composer's music, believes that Warren is acutely conscious of the level of quality she wishes to maintain and sees to it that only the best of her work is heard. Sensitive to the appropriate medium for any given text, Warren occasionally finds that a successful song can also make a successful choral piece; several of her vocal compositions have been published in both forms. She is frequently asked by publishers to set a choral piece for various combinations of voices. At the request of its publisher, she arranged her *Christmas Candle* for SATB accompanied and *a cappella*; men's chorus accompanied, women's chorus accompanied, in two editions - SA and SSA, and women's chorus SSAA *a cappella*.

A perfectionist, Warren will polish again and again and on one occasion completely revised a major composition, *Singing Earth*, to tighten its form. She re-orchestrated much of *The Harp Weaver* after its early performances, and laughingly refers to *The Legend of King Arthur* as her "life work." Even today, glancing over an old score of the choral symphony, she cannot resist "tinkering" with a phrase or two.

Early in her career, Elinor first ventured into the realm of the purely orchestral with the impressionistic short work *The Fountain*. This was followed, in 1946, by *The Crystal Lake*, a free-form tone poem which has proved to be one of her most frequently played orchestral compositions both here and in Europe.

With *The Crystal Lake*, Warren found a voice for her orchestral writing in the western landscapes so familiar to her. She, her husband, and eldest son came upon the lake after a rugged hike in California's High Sierras. *Crystal Lake* recreates the impression made upon her when suddenly, after climbing over ridges and snowfields, they discovered the secluded body of water, located near Lake Mary. Says Warren of the experience:

> Having heard about another lake on the mountaintop, in surroundings of rare beauty, we took a long hike to find it. It was in an isolated spot, 10,000 feet high, among the peaks where even in summer snow was still on the ground. There lay the Crystal Lake, sparkling and jewel-like, its waters lapping the shore, the wind in the pine trees, and one lone bird the only sounds to break the eerie stillness seldom interrupted by visitors.
>
> After our picnic lunch, a chill rain came briefly and drove us to shelter under the great boughs of the pine trees. Then as the skies cleared, the eternal peace and quiet beauty of the place was impressed deeply upon me again.

The work was given its West Coast premiere by the Los Angeles Philharmonic, conducted by Alfred Wallenstein, later conducted in New York and Canada by Wilfrid Pelletier and in Europe by Edouard van Remoortel. Andre Kostelanetz was to become one of its most enthusiastic champions; during the 1970's he conducted it widely throughout the United States. *The Crystal Lake's* many performances significantly contributed to Warren's being named, in a 1975 poll of America's major orchestras by *High Fidelity/Musical America,* one of the most performed women orchestral composers of the decade. This despite the fact that she had ignored economic realities and composed most of her works for large orchestra. In choosing this path, she was proceeding against the advice of colleagues who warned that numerous performances of new works for full orchestra, especially by a woman, would be virtually impossible.

But Warren's direction was instinctive. Some conductors complain that young composers do not know how to write for full orchestra; they have chosen to forego the medium, with its economic and rehearsal strictures. Warren, however, is consummately skilled in writing for full orchestra - one reason being her courage in continuing to pursue this form against all odds.

Besides Pelletier, Kostelanetz, Wallenstein, and van Remoortel, many other symphonic conductors of international stature, among them Hans Kindler, Henry Lewis, Antonia Brico, Pierre Monteux, Albert Coates, and Sir John Barbirolli, have conducted Warren works. Wallenstein, Pelletier, Kostelanetz, Coates, and Barbirolli became personal friends as well as admirers of the Warren musical output. Both Pelletier and Kostelanetz wrote frequently from New York and on tour, commenting upon the composer's scores which interested them. Alfred Wallenstein proved helpful in influencing Warren's thinking about orchestration. A former cellist in William Andrews Clark's first orchestra of 1919, he became the Los Angeles Philharmonic's permanent conductor in 1943. Having conducted world premieres of not only *The Crystal Lake* but another important Warren work, *Suite for Orchestra*, Wallenstein closely followed the composer's creative output. He invited her to attend his rehearsals with the orchestra and asked her to call him whenever she wished to discuss a musical problem. Wallenstein and his wife, Virginia, remained close to the Griffin family throughout the remainder of their lives.

In the preparation of her orchestral scores, Warren early found herself dissatisfied with the generally accepted method by which composers marked off clusters of measures by letter, to allow conductors and players a reference point when rehearsing. One of her copyists, Janet Guy, who had done work for the movie studios, suggested numbering each measure of a conductor's score instead of the system of periodic lettering. This method had been used extensively by film studio musicians; it offered a simple and effective means for conductor and players to quickly identify reference points. Warren believes she may have been one of the first to use this system in the field of serious music.

Absorbed with other projects, during the next eight years Elinor essayed only one work for orchestra, a short piece called *Scherzo*, which she orchestrated from an

early piano composition, *Frolic of the Elves*. Not until
1954 did she return to composing in this form. The
ensuing work was lengthier and more ambitious than any
she had yet written for orchestra. *Along the Western
Shore*, in three movements, is inspired by lines from the
American poets Edward Arlington Robinson, Robert Nathan
and Walt Whitman. Its first movement expresses musically
Robinson's words,

> Dark hills at evening in the West
> Where sunset hovers like a sound
> Of golden horns that sang to rest
> Old bones of warriors underground ...

The work's second movement incorporates the haunting
theme the composer had used in her earlier *Poem* for
viola, which later seemed to her evocative of Nathan's
lines,

> This is the country of the hungry heart
> This is the country where the noonday
> weather
> The scent of lilacs, of the summer night
> Can set us dreaming.

The third movement reflects Walt Whitman:

> Dashing spray, and the winds piping
> and blowing
> Fitful, like a surge.

With this work, Warren is again painting tone pictures of
landscapes she had come to know and love as a child
growing up in the West.

During the late 1940's and the decade that followed,
the composer's personal happiness and career successes
were to be shadowed by the loss of her parents. James
and Maude Warren had remained close to their daughter
after her marriage to Griffin, extending their love now to
include their son-in-law and a growing family of grandchildren. They had been married fifty-two years when, in
1949, James Warren died following a brief illness. Warren
was a warm man, filled with the joy of living; Elinor recalls that once, when she was a child, she saw him pick
up a small table and toss it into the air from sheer

exuberance. He had significantly influenced his daughter's musical direction.

Maude Warren survived for another decade. During these latter years she drew ever closer to Elinor, who as she had done from the beginning of her married life, either called or saw her mother almost every day. At the time of her death, Mrs. Warren was partially blind. The composer believes that years spent copying her music - "to save Elinor's eyes" - may have contributed to ruining her mother's sight. But that music had brought them a shared experience rare even for mother and daughter. To both parents Elinor gave the tribute of her finest work, dedicating "to my Mother and Father" her choral symphony *The Legend of King Arthur.*

6. INFLUENCES

In 1950, the Griffins purchased Rancho Corona del Valle, a 500-acre ranch in the High Sierras. Located on the slopes of Mt. Liebre, it overlooked vast reaches of the Mojave Desert and the southern range of the Sierra Nevadas. The ranch house and its several outbuildings, constructed as a hunting lodge by the father of one of Elinor's girlhood friends, had been built using adobe bricks made on the property.

It was Wayne Griffin's desire to purchase the ranch. At first his wife felt lukewarm about the idea; the place was run-down and the first time she visited it she had seen a scorpion in the bathtub and a snake crawling out of a couch.

Griffin and the enthusiastic children prevailed; the ranch became theirs. In addition to their own acreage, the new owners were granted the use for grazing of 300 additional acres of National Forest land at the top of Mt. Liebre. At first, Wayne Griffin experimented with raising turkeys, which he sold and shipped to wholesalers. When, however, dust from the 40,000 birds threatened to inundate the ranch house and its human inhabitants, Griffin switched to race horses, the raising of which became both hobby and business interest for the rest of his life. He achieved notable success; the Griffins' quarter-horse "Top Rockette" held the world championship for three years.

The composer, on her own mount, a Tennessee walking-horse named "Rambler," explored the Griffin ranchland during the family's weekend visits. In winter Elinor could look out across the Mojave to the High Sierras, blanketed with snow. In spring, she could see the wildflowers - orange, pink, white, yellow and purple - spread across the hills in giant patterns of brilliant color, as though an artist had been painting with an oversized brush. A true neo-Romantic, Warren has always looked to nature for revelation. The changing seasons, the pageantry of sunset, long shadows of towering mountains - these are moving experiences to her. Little wonder that she was to develop a profound attachment for this High Sierra territory, which from then on is reflected in much of her music.

During the 1950's, she was to find the inspiration for a major work, *Suite for Orchestra*, in the panorama of brilliant skies and cloud patterns surrounding Rancho Corona del Valle.

The *Suite* is conceived in four movements, Warren choosing lines from the poetry of John Gould Fletcher to introduce each movement and to reflect her own emotions about the scenes she has tried to paint into the music. In notes for the album cover of the CRI recording, the composer has written of her *Suite*:

> At our mountain ranch, we look out over broad sweeps of desert to the rugged snow-clad mountain ranges of the High Sierras. I have been particularly moved by the ever-changing pictures of the sky, at all hours, and in varying seasons. Although my *Suite* has no story or program behind it, the overtones of this pageantry of the sky and the long shadows of the towering mountains are doubtless [reflected] in the fabric of the work.

Suite for Orchestra was premiered in the spring of 1955 by the Los Angeles Philharmonic under Alfred Wallenstein, with performances soon after by the Montreal and Quebec Symphony Orchestras, conducted by Wilfrid Pelletier. Critics praised the work as "meriting a place in the standard orchestral repertoire" and noted its "telling use of an extensive instrumental palette." However in 1960, after her period of study in France with Nadia Boulanger, the composer made numerous changes in the orchestration; it is this later version that has been recorded by the Oslo Philharmonic for CRI.

The emotional influence of her mountain ranch no doubt contributed to an evolution that begins to appear in Warren's work with *Suite for Orchestra*. Never losing her neo-Romantic direction nor her idealism, she now infuses her music with a new passion. The other-worldly is increasingly subordinated to another of her major themes, nature. In virtually all of the orchestral compositions, as well as in songs such as *When You Walk Through Woods*, *Heather*, and *Sailing Homeward*, Warren has always expressed profound feeling for earth's natural wonders. However, works such as *Suite for Orchestra* and *Singing Earth* manifest heightened freedom and openness, exemplified in the dramatic interplay of mountain, sky, and forest which the composer witnessed repeatedly at Rancho Corona del Valle.

At this important period in her musical life, Warren finally made the decision to go to Paris for a concentrated period of study with Nadia Boulanger.

From 1921, when she first began teaching at the Conservatoire Américain at Fontainebleau, until her death at the age of 92 in 1979, Nadia Boulanger was the most influential musical pedagogue in the world. During the 1920's Georges Enesco had first suggested to Warren that she would enrich her musical expression by studying with Boulanger. Later, other musician friends had suggested the same; in each instance the time was not right. But during the 1950's the composer's close friends, conductor Wilfrid Pelletier and his wife, soprano Rose Bampton, again suggested that she go to Paris. By then Warren had achieved world recognition as a composer; Pelletier had conducted several of her major works and Bampton had given the first performance of her song *We Two* and premiered, at the 1952 Ojai Festival, her song cycle, *Singing Earth*. Bampton had also sung other Warren compositions in her concert and radio appearances. But regardless of the composer's already considerable reputation, Pelletier told Warren that to know Boulanger, to talk with her and absorb her ideas would be important for all future work. He had known Boulanger well when he lived in Paris; he promised to write her should Elinor make the decision to go.

Though realizing the value of Pelletier's suggestion, the composer found it difficult to think of leaving home and family for even the suggested few months. Yet the idea now seemed more feasible than formerly, since her children were older and away in school. When her husband enthusiastically seconded the Pelletiers' suggestion, Elinor decided this was the time to take advantage of the opportunity. After some correspondence with Boulanger, in early March of 1959, Warren embarked upon a three-month period of daily sessions with the famous teacher at the residence on Rue Ballu in Montmartre where she had lived for sixty years. Though the majority of Boulanger's pupils attended classes which she held every summer at Fontainebleau, Warren had private sessions with "Mademoiselle" while the teacher was in residence in Paris.

On the day of Warren's arrival, Boulanger decided to go out to the Paris airport in person, taking with her a gift of welcome for the well-known American composer who was to be her pupil. However, she went to the wrong airport and was not to meet Warren until the next day. Elinor recalls that Boulanger's attitude at their first meeting was somewhat abrupt, the teacher demanding to know why Warren, already a well-known composer, much performed and published, should want to study with her at this point in her career. Then she sharply criticized the American, who was about to cut a string that bound the score she had brought, scolding that one must never waste anything. Boulanger began to work open the knots in the string, taking precious time from the lesson while lecturing her new pupil on the virtues of string conservation rather than on music. Warren felt put off, and after the lesson told her husband, who had accompanied her to Paris for the first two weeks of her stay, that she had second thoughts about the plan. However she and Griffin finally found a small hotel, the Gallia, at 63, Rue Pierre-Charron, that would allow a piano; there she was to live and work during her time with Boulanger.

Each weekday and most Saturdays for the next three months - except for one lesson cancelled by Boulanger, who wanted to have her annual day in the country picking peas with friends - Warren and the celebrated teacher worked together. When she was not with Boulanger, the composer spent every moment attending concerts and opera and preparing material for her next day's session.

She had taken with her some specific compositions on which she wished to have Boulanger's advice; additionally, there was a new commission she wanted to work on while in Paris. However much of her time with the teacher was spent in conversation, and it is this which Warren feels to have been most valuable. The composer found Boulanger, then in her seventies, to be devoid of musical prejudices and very contemporary in her thinking. Besides offering her pupil new musical vistas, Boulanger was helpful technically with problems of orchestration - particularly in the balancing of voices within the orchestra and in choral writing.

The teacher who once said "In art there are no generations, only individuals; all times have been modern" encouraged musical experimentation by her pupils. Elinor made a conscious effort to write in a more *avant garde* style during this period of study, and her work with Boulanger marks an important transition which was to develop over the next fifteen years.

Before the composer returned home, Boulanger invited her to visit one of the renowned "Wednesday classes" held for pupils at her residence during the winter and spring months in Paris. There she insisted that Warren stand up and be introduced to the roomful of students. In front of the embarrassed American Boulanger exclaimed, "Now I want you to look at Elinor Warren! She has worked harder and accomplished more this spring than any of the rest of you have in a whole year!"

By then, the two had developed a warm and close friendship. Boulanger's personal and professional regard for Warren is expressed in this letter, written shortly after the American's departure: "You have left here what can never be destroyed - and I am happy to know you well by now, for all that you are in your spirit, your heart and your dignity. It shows in your work as it shows in your life - and I thank the Lord for your coming."

The friendship continued until Boulanger's death. The teacher wrote frequently, never forgetting Elinor's birthdays and wedding anniversaries. When the Griffins traveled to Europe they always went to Paris for a visit with "Mademoiselle"; in 1967, they were present in Monte Carlo to celebrate Boulanger's eightieth birthday at a memorable concert and party hosted by Prince Rainier and Princess Grace.

Following her return from the Paris sojourn with Boulanger, Warren and her husband decided to take their children out of school for a semester of travel - just as Elinor at the age of twelve had been taken on an extended tour of Europe. The Griffins were gone from December of 1959 through March of 1960, traveling around the world.

Once back in the States, the composer again felt the urge to revise several earlier compositions. Among these was her cycle for voice and orchestra, *Singing Earth*, which had premiered in 1952 at the Ojai Festival with Rose Bampton as soprano soloist and Thor Johnson conducting - the sole work by an American to be presented at the 1952 Festival. Shortly thereafter the work was performed in Vienna and then in Greece, at the first program of American music ever heard in Athens. The concert took place in the Herodicus Atticus amphitheatre at the base of the Acropolis, with Metropolitan Opera soprano Nadine Conner as soloist with the Athens Symphony Orchestra. Athens critics were complimentary, saying the work was "the best composition which has been presented in recent times by a representative of the fair sex" and it "surely constituted the climax of the evening." Though on both occasions the composer was fortunate in having *Singing Earth* performed by distinguished soloists and excellent orchestras, when she studied a tape sent her of the Athens performance she felt dissatisfied with some aspects of the composition. Warren has said, "One learns so much from hearing into the music. You can go down to a beautiful stream and look at it, but it is different after you wade into the water. Every composer knows how he or she wants a work to sound, but sometimes hearing it performed gives a different impression."

Believing the orchestral sections between the four poems of the cycle to be overly long and the orchestration in need of more work, she withdrew *Singing Earth* from further performance, intending to revise it as soon as practicable. But because the "leave of absence" in Paris had involved her in many other musical projects, and because she works slowly and introspectively, it was not until the end of the 1970's that she found time to make her long-planned revisions.

Singing Earth was originally written as a four-song cycle for soprano and piano, though Warren always had an orchestration in mind. This was the first of the composer's two major works set to poems by Carl Sandburg. It seemed inevitable that she should be attracted to the writings of this poet with a strong rhythmic cadence to his words and an affinity for the land, specifically the rough splendor of the American wilderness and the sprawling cities that have sprung from it.

The four poems of *Singing Earth* - *The Wind Sings Welcome*, *Summer Stars*, *Tawny Days*, and *Great Memories* - were chosen by Warren from various Sandburg collections. Her sense that they belonged together she explained to the poet upon their first meeting. Sandburg was in Los Angeles for a poetry reading and invited her to come with a singer to the house where he was staying to sing for him the four song sections. Sandburg agreed that the poems did go well together, though he had never before thought of it.

As he listened to the music the poet sat unnervingly close to the soprano, focusing intently on her face, saying nothing between songs. But at the conclusion, he slapped his knee and remarked delightedly, "Now I know why I wrote them!"

Sandburg closely followed the progress of this composition, remarking to Warren in a letter, "A fellow looks with keen interest in what of his work is chosen for musical setting. I think of you as a good friend." From his Connemara Farms in North Carolina, he wrote offering his suggestions of a title for the cycle: "*Earth Singing* or *Wind, Stars, and Sea* occur to me as possible titles, but perhaps these thoughts may lead you to a title of your own you will like better." A shift of Sandburg's wording suited the composer, and *Singing Earth* it became. Later, when Warren sent him a recording of the orchestral setting of the cycle, the poet replied - prophetically as it was to turn out: "The record is profound and subtle and I salute you. I like to think of your constant work in 'The

American grain' ..." He did not live long enough to hear his poetry in another of her major compositions - one decidedly in "the American grain" - *Good Morning, America!*

Warren believes that her musical output of this period and beyond tends to portray a wider vision. Criticizing herself for an early tendency to over-orchestrate, she affirms that her orchestral expression was later tempered by more knowledge of technique. In *Singing Earth* she balances passionate expression and technique to create some of her most successful writing - writing so closely mirroring Sandburg's mood pictures that poet and composer seem inextricably linked.

A 1976 article on Warren by Los Angeles radio personality Carl Princi notes "As a result of only a very few meetings with Elinor Remick Warren it was unusually simple to recognize a personal charm which seems to radiate through your own person simply by shaking her hand. She is a person who exudes warmth, friendliness and sincerity ..." Indeed, upon being introduced to the composer one is instantly aware of a nature at once open and intuitive, eager to pour out ideas and feelings. Never have those qualities of Warren's personality translated themselves to her music more effectively than in *Singing Earth*. As she had begun to do in *Suite for Orchestra*, she now breaks past technical challenges and emotional constraints, as the songs contrast with each other and flow from one to the next without interruption - a device rarely heard in song cycles. At the last comes a building of orchestral and vocal forces, as the music seems to hurl itself toward its climax.

By the late 1940's, Wayne Griffin had left his position as head of the radio department of BBDO to join the Berg-Allenberg Agency, representing their stars in radio. One of these stars was Charles Laughton. It was Griffin who interested Laughton in the one-man stage readings from the Bible which were later to add greatly to Laughton's fame. At first the actor was unsure of himself in this new theatrical path; he spent many evenings at the Griffin home, reading the Bible for his first audience - Wayne's and Elinor's children. Eventually Laughton felt sure enough to advance to the next stage -

an appearance at the Griffins' church. Finally, he held his "graduation" reading at young Jim Griffin's school. The rest is theatrical history.

Griffin later went into independent film production. For his first film, *Family Honeymoon*, starring Fred MacMurray and Claudette Colbert, he accomplished what no one before him had been able to do: he persuaded the U.S. Department of the Interior to lease him the Grand Canyon for location filming.

Griffin's later films were to star such screen luminaries as Ava Gardner, Lionel Barrymore, Loretta Young, and Clark Gable. Though increasingly well-known as a producer of successful films, Griffin remained generally apart from the Hollywood social scene. One of his and his wife's few close personal friends from the film colony was Gable, who often visited at Rancho Corona del Valle. Once, the Griffins and Gable were vacationing together in New York when the three decided to attend a Broadway show. Photographers rushed to take the star's picture as he entered the theatre beside the "unknown" blonde beauty; at the same time, they mistook Griffin for Cary Grant. Elinor was often mistaken for movie star Janet Gaynor, to whom she bore an uncanny resemblance; she was frequently besieged on Los Angeles streets by Gaynor's fans asking for autographs. The composer's only foray into films was not musical: Gable once persuaded her and her husband to appear with him as "extras" in the restaurant scene of a forgettable film, *Callaway Went Thataway*.

Besides Gable and Nelson Eddy, the Griffins' other close friends from films were Jeanette MacDonald and her husband, Gene Raymond. Along with their movie careers, MacDonald and Eddy individually made many tours throughout the United States in concerts of the classical repertoire. Jeanette MacDonald added to Warren's fame by singing her songs, among them *Heather* and *Down in the Glen*, Eddy with his programming of *Remembering*, *Sweetgrass Range* and the song Warren wrote for him, *To the Farmer*. For five years Ann and Nelson Eddy were the Griffins' neighbors. Nelson enthusiastically participated in touch football games played with the Griffin children up and down the street. One year while on tour he and his wife found an antique mug which they presented to the composer upon their return. On it was the anonymous early English poem which she used as her text for *To the Farmer.*

Richard and Mildred Crooks had come to Los Angeles to live following his retirement from the concert stage, and the Griffins saw them often. Both couples had always delighted in each other's humor. One January, when he was still singing at the Metropolitan Opera, Crooks appeared as Des Grieux opposite Grace Moore's Manon on a live Saturday afternoon radio broadcast of the Massenet opera. Afterwards, Elinor telegraphed him from Los Angeles:

> Here's to Crooks who sings like a bird,
> From Coast-to-Coast his tenor is heard.
> His B-flat rings like a chime in the tower,
> With his pear-shaped tones he's the man
>   of the hour.
> As the noble Des Grieux opposite la Moore
> He has his countrymen swingin' -
>   especially Wayne and *Elinoor.*

Crooks replied, also by wire:

> Thanks for the wire, we liked it a lot,
> Am terribly glad Manon sounded hot.
> Even tho' I swooned and fell on the floor
> The gal that went with me was Gracie La
>   Moore.
> The old year hath passed, the new year is in
> The Crooks' send their love to the family
>   Griffin.

Upon its publication during the early 1930's, Warren added Edna St. Vincent Millay's volume of narrative sonnets, *Fatal Interview,* to her large poetry collection. *Fatal Interview* is a poignant, compelling group of fifty-two poems; from the first the composer had wanted to set some of them as a cycle. Though she chose four - Sonnets 7, 11, 35, and 52 - for use in the projected work, the music remained in sketch form for many years.

It was not until the early 1950's that Warren, looking over this earlier work, decided to develop her ideas for

it. Feeling the deeply moving poems to be particularly
suited to voice with strings, she called the thirteen-
minute work *Sonnets for Soprano and String Quartet*. Its
first performance took place in 1954 at the Los Angeles
County Museum of Art, with the Musart String Quartet
and soprano Patricia Beems. Warren also adapted the work
for soprano and string orchestra. This version was premiered at UCLA's Royce Hall in a concert of the National
Association of Composers U.S.A. Reviewing the performance, Albert Goldberg of the *Los Angeles Times* noted
the work's "long spun, admirable vocal melodies set
against a sensitive and expressive harmonic background -
a valuable addition to the song literature." Though this is
one of only a few chamber works by the composer, it has
proven to be among her most enduring larger compositions,
performed frequently here and abroad.

In early 1958, the Board of Directors of the
Hollywood Bowl asked Warren to write a theme for the
chimes, to be played just before concerts and at inter-
missions, indicating to audiences the music's beginning and
its resumption. Though it was a departure from anything
she had written before, Warren found herself intrigued
with the idea. During the 1958 Hollywood Bowl season her
sixteen measures were heard for the first time, played
once on the carillon, then with full orchestra and the
Roger Wagner Chorale singing the melody line.

Later, after completion of the Dorothy Chandler
Pavilion at the Los Angeles Music Center, the *Carillon
Theme* was also played there for the same purpose at
every concert. Played continuously since 1959, the melody
has been heard thousands of times by audiences attending
musical events.

During a visit to Los Angeles, one of the composer's
publishers went with the Griffins to Hollywood Bowl.
Believing that her melody would lend itself for singing on
patriotic, graduation, and other special occasions, he suggested that Warren enlarge upon the *Carillon Theme* and
write it as a chorus. Never able to find a text that will
fit an already-written composition, Warren, in desperation,
penned words of her own, for which she used the
pseudonym Samuel Bonner. She added another sixteen
measures to the composition and it became *Our Beloved*

Land, published in 1963 for mixed chorus and piano or orchestra. The full composition received its premiere at Hollywood Bowl August 10, 1963, with the Jack Halloran Singers and John Scott Trotter conducting the Hollywood Bowl Orchestra.

By the early 1960's, the Griffins' children were in college. Wayne Griffin had by now made a number of successful films, but he believed that for the moment the days of the independent film producer were waning. Though he had also involved himself with television during the 1950's, producing *GE Theatre* hosted by Ronald Reagan, Griffin now felt it necessary to devote full time to the business responsibilities left him by his father-in-law. Moreover, the raising of quarter-horses, begun as a hobby, had developed into a major enterprise. Griffin now began another career: as businessman and civic leader. So successful became this new direction that by 1970 his business interests were widespread and he was serving on thirty-five prominent boards, particularly distinguishing himself as Director of the Los Angeles Community Redevelopment Agency.

Two important careers in the family never created a conflict for Wayne and Elinor, both being intensely interested in each other's activities. About his devotion to music, Griffin said in an interview during this period, "It led me to the best thing that ever happened to me - my wife!"

In the 1960's, Warren returned to the large canvasses of early career successes such as *The Harp Weaver* and *The Legend of King Arthur*. At the same time she continued, as she has throughout her life, writing for solo voice and for chorus - *a cappella* or with piano or organ. Her shorter choral works, for mixed, women's or men's chorus, are based on both secular and religious texts. Some, originally written for solo voice, were performed so widely that publishers requested her to arrange them for chorus also. At this time, the recital field was declining in America and music publishing houses had begun to show less interest in solos and more in choral music. This proved no hindrance for Warren; from her earliest career her choral works had found ready publication.

Since the mid-1930's, America has rivaled Great Britain in the number and quality of its choral groups. Both civic and university-based, these groups frequently program Warren compositions.

One of the California-based college choruses which has achieved special distinction is that of Occidental College. Dr. Howard Swan, its director for many years, gained extraordinary results with the young singers he trained, and he became nationally renowned as a choral director. Swan, a champion of Warren's choral music, finds it "so appropriate for the voice." His singing groups - men's and women's glee clubs and large combined chorus - have programmed virtually every published choral composition by Warren. This has allowed her to hear the works in performance, thus to perfect details of interpretation that could most clearly be perceived in that way. Swan's association with her choral output proved a broadening experience for the composer and she went on to produce some of her most successful compositions in this medium: among them *Night Rider*, a mixed choral work of strong rhythms and a quality of mystery; *Time, You Old Gypsy-Man*, also a chorus for mixed voices, that expresses a rugged quality in its vigorous accompaniment and exuberant vocal lines; *Songs for Young Voices*, set to poems which she recited to her grandchildren while playing with them in the garden during visits; and *To My Native Land*, one of four of her choral compositions based on themes of Americana, the others being *Our Beloved Land*, *Good Morning, America!* and *Transcontinental*.

Transcontinental, completed in 1958, was written for Swan's mixed chorus, with baritone soloist, and was given its premiere at Occidental with orchestra. Its text, by A.M. Sullivan, conducts listeners by train on a tour across the United States. Published before air travel had become universal, *Transcontinental* received many performances. Now, with a renewal of interest in trains as a way of seeing the country, it should again find new audiences.

During the 1950's, Warren's stature had grown to such proportions that she now began receiving commissions which intrigued her more than formerly. Some of these she did not accept, being involved with other compositions and intent on guarding her freedom to write what appealed to her most strongly. When approached with a commission to compose music for a new ballet, she declined, feeling she did not possess sufficient understanding of the ballet form. Though she had maintained a lifelong attraction for both the vocal and dramatic arts, she also did not succumb to urgings to write an opera, never finding the libretto that would inspire her enough to write in a form where opportunities for performances are scarce. However, before she went to Paris for study with Nadia Boulanger, Warren was contacted by the well-known Chicago baritone, businessman and music patron Louis Sudler, who proposed an unusual commission. Sudler, who performed often as soloist with the Chicago Symphony and scored a great success singing *King Arthur's Farewell* on his many concert tours, had learned that one of the Dead Sea Scrolls had recently been unearthed and brought to Israeli archaeologists after they thought their collection of the parchments to be complete. Upon translation from the ancient Aramaic, the newly-discovered scroll proved to be very significant. It provided an extended and more colorful version of the story of *Abram and Sarai* than that more briefly related in the Book of Genesis, revealing, for example, the dream which caused Abram to urge the beautiful Sarai to conceal her true identity as his wife.

Sudler wanted a large work for baritone and orchestra based on writings from the scroll. Excited at having been given the opportunity of working on such a project, Warren first carefully studied both Genesis and texts of the parchments, titled The Genesis Apocryphon. The latter had been translated but not yet published. She discovered the text to be far more poetic than the more factual account in Genesis and realized that combining the texts would fill out the story. Thus, she selected portions of each writing for her projected composition. However, as the scroll's narrative is written in the first person, she found it necessary to change some of the Genesis excerpts from third person to first. The composer's skill in melding these texts is evident upon a study of Warren's final draft, with scroll columns and verses indicated:

> **GENESIS** Now there was a famine in the land. So Abram went down to Egypt to

sojourn there, for the famine was severe in the land.

SCROLLS, COLUMN XIX "I, Abram, dreamed a dream on the night of our entering into the land of Egypt.

"I woke from my slumber that night and said to Sarai, my wife, 'A dream have I dreamt ... [18] and I am frightened by this dream.' And she said to me, 'Tell me thy dream, that I may know.' And I began to tell her; [14] Lo! I saw in my dream one cedar tree and one palm, [15] and men came and sought to cut down and uproot the cedar, and to leave the palm by itself. [16] The palm cried out and said, Cut not down the cedar, for cursed is he who will fell it. And for the sake of the palm the cedar was saved.

GENESIS "I know that you are a woman beautiful to behold; and when the Egyptians see you, they will say, 'This is his wife': then they will kill me, but they will let you live. Say you are my sister, that my life may be spared on your account.

SCROLLS [21] "And Sarai wept at my words that night."

GENESIS When Abram entered Egypt, the princes of Pharaoh saw that Sarai was very beautiful, and they praised her to Pharaoh.

SCROLLS, COLUMN XX [2] "How beautiful the look of her face, and how [3] fine is the hair of her head; how fair indeed are her eyes, and all the radiance [4] of her face. Her arms goodly to look upon, and her hands, [5] how perfect! [6] Above all [7] women is she lovely, and higher is her beauty than that of them all. And with all her beauty there is much wisdom in her."

[8] When the King heard these words, he sent [9] at once to bring her to him.

[10] "And I wept, [11] with grievous weeping, wept that night when Sarai was taken from me by force.

[12] "That night I prayed and entreated in sorrow, as my tears fell; [13] 'Behold now [14] I cry before Thee, my Lord, against Pharaoh-Zoan, King of Egypt, because my wife has been taken from me by force. Do Thou judge him for me and let me behold Thy mighty hand [15] descend upon him and all his household.' [16] And I wept and grieved."

That night the Most High God sent a pestilential wind to afflict Pharaoh and all his household, a wind that [17] was evil. And it smote him and all his house, and he could not come near Sarai.

[19] Then Pharaoh called for all the wise men of Egypt and all the wizards, if perchance they might heal him, him and [20] his house [19] from the pestilence. [20] And all the wizards and wise men could not rise up to heal him, for the wind smote them all, [21] and they fled. [18] The plagues and the afflictions became grievous and strong! [21] "Then came a Prince of Pharaoh and besought me to come and pray for [22] the king, that he might live. And I said, 'I cannot pray [23] for the King while Sarai, my wife, is with him. Go now, and tell the King to send away my wife, and I will pray for him, and he will live!'"

GENESIS "So Pharaoh called me, and said, 'What is this you have done to me? Why did you not tell me Sarai was your wife?'

"'I did it,' I said, 'because I thought, there is no fear of God at all in this place, and they will kill me because of my wife. So I said to Sarai, 'At every place where we come, say of me, *He is my brother!*'"

Then Pharaoh said, SCROLLS [27] "Behold now thy wife! GENESIS Take her SCROLLS [27] go thy way, and depart from all the land of Egypt. And now, pray for me and all my house, that this evil wind may depart from us!"

"And I prayed, [29] and the plague departed from him and the evil wind was gone, and he lived!"

GENESIS Pharaoh gave orders concerning us; they set us on our way, with all that we had.

Then the Lord said, "Lift up your eyes, and look from the place where you are, northward and southward, eastward and westward. Arise, and walk through the length and breadth of the land, for I will give it to you and your descendants, forever!"

As she contemplated her projected composition, which at first she called *Abram and Sarai*, Warren decided it demanded a chorus as well as a soloist. She offered to return Sudler's commission stipend should he disagree with her conception. He did not, but requested also a version for solo baritone and orchestra without chorus, which Warren agreed to write.

In Paris during the spring of 1959, the composer spent some of her sessions with Boulanger gaining the teacher's advice about the construction and orchestration of certain phases of the work. Back in Los Angeles, working throughout the summer, she completed details of the composition, for chorus, baritone and orchestra.

Abram in Egypt combines modal influences and a modern idiom. With this composition - completed after her study in Paris - the composer begins her move away from a strictly neo-Romantic expression. Warren has said of *Abram*: "It is quite different from my other works, more angular. Although I have not specifically used any ancient Hebraic themes in this music, my thinking has been influenced by the ancient text."

Louis Sudler premiered the version for solo voice and orchestra April 19, 1959, in a performance at Northwestern University, Thor Johnson conducting. A *tour de force* for baritone, who must carry the entire twenty-two minute story vocally, it proved a challenging but successful endeavor for the singer, and he subsequently performed the work in other concert appearances. The choral version of *Abram and Sarai*, now retitled by the composer *Abram in Egypt*, was chosen in 1961 to receive its world premiere at the first Los Angeles International Music Festival, held at UCLA. For this first performance, also broadcast throughout the world on Voice of America, Roger Wagner conducted the Festival Orchestra and the Los Angeles Master Chorale, with Metropolitan Opera baritone Donald Gramm as soloist. The new cantata, presented June 7, 1961, was well-received upon this important occasion, reviewers writing of its "splendor and amplitude of sound," and noting "Its idiom stemmed from tradition, but there was freedom and unconventionality in its exercise." *Abram in Egypt* provided the festival with its only premiere; that night it followed works by Darius Milhaud, Roy Harris and Ian Hamilton, each composer present to conduct his own composition. Warren appeared as panelist in a symposium held during the ten-day event. Answering questions put to her and the other participating composers by audience members, she argued that a composer must first master technique before achieving freedom of expression. Fourteen distinguished composers from the United States, Russia, Sweden, Germany, Mexico, England and France - among them Milhaud, Harris and Hamilton, as well as Igor Stravinsky, Blas Galindo, Walter Piston, Lukas Foss, John Vincent, Franz Waxman and Miklos Rozsa - gathered at Los Angeles to hear their works performed during the Festival. Warren was the only woman represented.

Two years after the International Music Festival had taken place in Los Angeles, Roger Wagner approached the composer with a commission for a new work. Long a champion of Warren's music, the celebrated conductor had, in turn, contributed significantly to Warren's growth as a composer of choral music. A native of France, Wagner possessed a supreme understanding of the literature for both organ and chorus. Warren admired his musicianship and believes that attendance at his rehearsals with the Los Angeles Master Chorale taught her much about writing for chorus - what is "singable," how words and music are projected, the various effects that can be achieved.

Wagner frequently programmed Warren's shorter compositions on his nationwide concert tours and on his tours of South America, Europe, the Near East, and the U.S.S.R. In addition to *Abram in Egypt*, he had also programmed another of the composer's major works, *The Harp Weaver*, with the women's group of his Chorale, and in 1954 - deciding Los Angeles should hear it a second time - had presented *The Legend of King Arthur* on his concert series at Philharmonic Auditorium. For this performance Wagner conducted the Los Angeles Master Chorale and Sinfonia Orchestra, with Metropolitan Opera baritone Robert Weede and tenor William Olvis as soloists. Young Chorale members Patricia Beems, Phyllis Wilkins and Marilyn Horne sang the Three Queens. Though nearly fifteen years had elapsed since last they heard it, Los Angeles music reviewers were as enthusiastic as previously, praising Warren's dramatic power and saying the work had "more than fulfilled in performance the high expectations it had aroused from the earlier hearing ... It was an occasion that fully warranted the audience's cheers that followed it."

Wagner now suggested that the composer accept his commission to write a Requiem. Thinking of the sublime compositions already extant in this genre and being unfamiliar with the Catholic liturgy, at first she hesitated. But Wagner insisted she would find it an inspiring and broadening experience, one she should not pass up; Warren later acknowledged this to have been good advice. Once having decided to accept the commission, she immediately set to work.

Creating her *Requiem* proved to be a deeply religious experience for the composer. Though she is reticent about articulating her personal religious beliefs, Warren's work reveals deep spiritual wellsprings. She maintains that the dedication and prayer expended upon the writing of this composition - over a period of three years of intense concentration - changed her life. "It was a growth experience" she says, "engrossing and monumental. I think of a Requiem not only as a service for one person's death, but as a monument of faith, which evolved from thirteenth century liturgical prayers; prayers for all mankind to a loving God. It reemphasizes man's faith and his belief that a righteous life leads to life everlasting."

A Requiem offers the composer much diversity in his or her choice of what and how much of the liturgy to use. Warren spent weeks in libraries, studying liturgical forms and the history involved in their development, to better understand the full meaning and character of the subject before developing a musical/liturgical concept emphasizing Christianity's positive hope of resurrection and the love of a forgiving God. Thus, the Warren *Requiem* comprises an *Introit*, *Kyrie*, *Graduale*, *Dies Irae*, *Offertorium*, *Hostias*, *Sanctus*, *Benedictus* and *Hosanna*, and *Agnus Dei*, ending with the *Lux Aeterna*. As with *Abram in Egypt*, the composer prepared her own English text. However, the work may also be performed in Latin, which Warren prefers.

The 53-minute composition, when completed, comprised a piano-vocal published edition, and the score for orchestra, chorus, soprano and baritone soloists. Though originally the female solo had been written for mezzo-soprano, before the premiere Warren rewrote the part for soprano.

During the three years she spent writing the *Requiem*, Warren fortified herself with afternoon coffee - the only time she has ever done so - to keep going through the long, intensive work hours. Only when she heard the bell of the local ice cream vendor, who came down her street just before six p.m. each day, did she stop working, knowing her husband would then be on the way home from his office.

Requiem, by Elinor Remick Warren, was premiered at the new Dorothy Chandler Pavilion of the Los Angeles Music Center on April 3, 1966, with Roger Wagner conducting the Los Angeles Master Chorale and Sinfonia Orchestra, soprano Carol Neblett and baritone Paul Hinshaw as soloists. As has nearly always been the case with Warren's major compositions, reviews were gratifying. The *Los Angeles Herald Examiner* called the work, "a dignified, meditative, distinguished contribution to choral literature," while *Los Angeles Times* music critic Martin

Bernheimer hailed its composer as an "undeniable mistress of her *metier*." The *Sanctus* section of the work, published separately, is sung widely. Wagner, who believes it to be "one of [Warren's] finest efforts," programmed it on a long nationwide tour, on a State Department tour of the Near East and Europe, and later during a tour of South America. For the latter, Warren provided an arrangement for chorus and strings, with organ or piano.

With *Requiem* the composer again attains the spiritual heights she first scaled in *The Legend of King Arthur*. This is music striving for a perfection beyond man and his passions, a view entirely appropriate in light of the portions of the Mass she chose to set. However, the *Dies Irae - Day of Wrath -* with its tension and forebodings of death, was included by the composer to provide what she felt to be an important musical contrast to the more contemplative and exalted sections of the rest of the work. Warren ends her *Requiem* quietly, with sustained chords in muted brass and strings that seem all the more powerful for the quality they evoke of peace and worshipful reflection.

At a mid-way point in her career, Warren, perhaps for an interview or contemplated article, jotted some notes on being a composer. "One must be prepared," she wrote, "for a life of frequent periods of isolation, with no interruptions of the concentration required to attack the blank sheet of manuscript staring back from the work table. Don't plan on going out to lunch," she warns. "You will rarely see even the friends dear to your heart. No phone calls, either, to break the concentration." Only in the evenings did she and her husband visit with friends.

In a 1957 interview, she touched upon this same theme when recalling Carl Sandburg's words to her as they discussed *Singing Earth* together. In the poet's opinion, the danger of the times was that there was no leisure for thinking, and he added, "How can one listen to the inner voice except in aloneness?" Feeling that music can "go farther, higher, deeper than the written or spoken word," Warren has accepted the strictures imposed upon her by her career. "Each of us," she says, "has so much to work out alone. After we learn the basic principles of any phase of life, then we must go on alone, working out the individual interpretation." She believes one cannot be taught how to compose; "the impulse is there from the beginning." One can, however, be given the "grammar" - theory, form, techniques, and the criticisms of an objective teacher. But the student must guard against imitating the mentor.

"Write what you *feel*" Warren remarked in some notes of advice for young composers, "not what you think a publisher wants." To this ideal she has remained faithful, regardless of the revolutionary winds that have swept many a contemporary, however unwillingly, toward atonalism. She regrets that a composer is expected to spend precious time aiding the publisher in promoting his or her works with performers and conductors. Such effort disturbs the concentration needed for creative work. Moreover, it presupposes that the composer is acquainted with the performer or conductor being approached, since it is sometimes through such personal contacts that a work is placed on a busy orchestra's performance schedule.

Warren also deplores the treatment often accorded a serious composer by conductors and/or performers who ignore query letters, or keep a requested score more than a year - sometimes losing it in the process. Publishers often wait months to read and decide upon a submitted composition and, once having decided, may take two years or more getting it into print. There is also the occasional publisher who periodically shreds for tax purposes all published copies of compositions remaining in stock, without giving their composers the chance of recovering the music. Warren refers to her profession as "my luxury," for the difficulties of getting works published and performed are compounded by the original costs to the composer involved in copying, photocopying, binding and mailing scores - costs hardly offset by the relatively small royalties earned even by successful serious works. The composer must then depend on other sources - money available from grants, foundations, and competitions - to cover these expenses. "There's so much more than the inspiration of writing a composition," she adds. "You must take time from composing just to handle the logistics and details involved in producing a score." Warren has written of the emotions involved in composing music; the exhilaration she experiences upon completing a work. "I then like to put it away for a while, so I may look at it more objectively later. Finally, I go over it again, often rewriting details or sometimes whole sections." When involved in a new composition, she becomes so absorbed that all her other works fade into the background. Composition is at once "frustrating and satisfying" - frustrating because "you are called upon to create something out of nothing," satisfying because "once you have done so, it is there!"

She maintains the reasons she is a composer are "elusive and difficult to pinpoint;" it would appear to have been "a compulsion" which gripped her early. "I had this music in my head and I had no choice about it - I simply had to keep writing it." Regardless, she admits she would not advise young people to assume the enormous sacrifices required if composition of serious music is to be the sole means of support. Nonetheless, she has established a scholarship at Occidental College to aid young musicians of the future. And she is fond of quoting words by Robert Frost that express her feelings about her own career, the intense work and dedication that have gone into it:

> My object in living is to unite
> My avocation and my vocation
> As my two eyes make one in sight.

The mid and latter '60's brought added happiness into the composer's personal life as she saw her children marry and begin families of their own. In 1965, Wayne, Jr. married Cynthia Niven and in 1967, daughter Elayne became Mrs. Thomas Techentin. Jim has remained a bachelor, and all three live in the Los Angeles area. The Griffin Jrs. were to present the composer with her first grandchild, Zachary Wayne III, born in 1966; two years later came Timothy Griffin. There would follow three other grandchildren, born to the Techentin family: Warren, Kristin and Nicholas. Elinor's house once again echoed with the welcome sound of youngsters, as grandchildren came for frequent visits. The expanded family was often together on weekends at the ranch and on family trips.

In 1969, Warren was honored by the New York Public Library in its exhibit "Contemporary Women Composers in the United States," arranged in recognition of the 75th anniversary of the International Council of Women and the National Council of Women in the United States. Ten leading American women composers were featured with an exhibit of their scores, photographs, programs and biographical sketches. Besides Warren, others singled out for recognition included Miriam Gideon, Louise Talma, Vivian Fine, Gena Branscombe and Julia Smith. In anticipation of the exhibit, New York radio station WNYC held its 30th annual Festival of American Music, honoring the composers featured in the exhibit. Warren's *Sonnets for Soprano and String Quartet* was heard at the Festival, and its composer made the wire services, Associated Press carrying her comment at the concert: "They tell me they're paying me the highest compliment when they say, after a performance of one of my works, 'Why, it sounds as if it was written by a man!'"

That comment had plagued Warren from the beginning. As a very young girl, she had sold numerous songs to a well-known New York music publisher. They had never met until one day she decided to stop in to his office. Shocked, he scrutinized her. "But however can you write such strong, masculine music when you look like this?"

The appearance is deceptive. About her work Warren is forceful and positive. She is, moreover, possessed of a deeply emotional nature; one that has been powerfully directed into her musical output. It is this emotional power that is mistaken by the listener - conditioned through centuries to think of men creating music - as "masculine." Like a fine actress, Warren, through her empathy with a text or her own sense memory, is able to create whatever mood she deems appropriate. She maintains that music has no gender, yet she admits:

> It's strange, but people just don't expect a woman's work to be as strong as a man's. They listen to it differently, or perhaps not at all. Even I, who have been more fortunate than many, often thought it might have been wise to have followed a friend's advice years ago and signed my works as 'E. Warren,' or maybe even 'Remick Warren.'

In another interview on the subject she adds:

> I believe people do think of a composer as being a man. If it's a woman, they're liable to think she isn't serious. That she dashes off a little song or something in her spare time.

Elinor and Wayne celebrated their thirtieth wedding anniversary on December 12, 1966, with a gala party Wayne planned as a surprise for his wife. Shared by all their friends, the celebration was capped for the composer by her husband's toast to her: "When I wake up in the morning, I wake up with a smile, because there is Elinor - my sunshine."

Shortly thereafter, the Griffins were invited to attend another surprise event: Nadia Boulanger's eightieth birthday party in Monaco, hosted by Prince Rainier and Princess Grace. Invitations to the 500 guests cautioned "*Garde le secret*," and so everyone did. The Griffins had a happy reunion with "Mademoiselle" at the gala, September 30, 1967, following a festive concert conducted by Igor Markevitch and featuring as soloists Yehudi Menuhin and Mattiwilda Dobbs, with the Orchestre de Monte Carlo.

Wayne had known Princess Grace during her years in Hollywood. The following afternoon the Griffins were invited to the palace for tea, with only the Rainiers and Boulanger present. At the royal children's supper time, Elinor was amused to see the youngsters in their pajamas coming to wish everyone goodnight.

As her birthday gift, Boulanger was presented with a large portfolio of works created for her by her distinguished creative friends - artists, musicians and writers who had known and loved her. Warren wrote a song for her. The message she sent with it reveals the depth of her regard: "Dear Mlle. Nadia - May I add my small tribute in music as a birthday offering, along with so many more you will receive ... Your influence upon music, and upon the hearts and lives of all who know you cannot be measured, and we have come from far and near to honor you at this happy time. May your skies be clear and bright, as you continue to help others up those steep hills you have surmounted by your wisdom, your faith, and your loving heart ..." Thoughtful and affectionate, Boulanger responded by personal letter to all the many birthday tributes.

These were the years for laurels, though earlier, in 1953, the *Los Angeles Times* had presented the composer with its coveted Woman of the Year award. And in 1954, Warren had been given an honorary Doctor of Music degree from Occidental College. The citation, presented by her valued friend and colleague, Dr. Howard Swan, paid tribute to "a woman who is one of America's outstanding composers; who possesses the companion qualities of persistent industry and creative zeal. Furthermore, this combination of excellencies is possessed by a woman of loveliness, of grace and of great personal charm."

Each year since 1959, Warren has received an ASCAP award "for significant contribution to the cultural growth and enrichment of our nation's musical heritage." The composer has been a member of ASCAP since 1936, and this award is offered annually to members of the Society whose catalogs "have a unique prestige value."

Having been elected a Life Member of the National Federation of Music Clubs, in 1972, Warren was further honored with an entire program of her works at the Annual Convention of the National Association of Teachers of Singing. The latter group named her "Composer of the Decade for 1976." Two other important honors came during the '70's. In June of 1975, *High Fidelity/Musical America* magazine asked five major orchestras what works by women had been performed by them during the past decade. Elinor Remick Warren headed the list with five performances of her orchestral works by three of the five orchestras polled: Detroit, New York, and Los Angeles. Warren works had been programmed by the latter more than those of any other woman composer, with a total of six works during a span of nearly three decades.

Throughout her career, the composer has foregone grants and competitions, feeling she should leave the field to those who so often need the additional financial backing. Only once did she enter a major competition, and she was a prize-winner. In 1961, *Abram in Egypt* was awarded second prize in the vocal category of the Gedok International Competition for Women Composers held at Mannheim, Germany. Having just completed the work, Warren impulsively decided to enter it.

Upon reflection, the composer considers it may have been unwise to forego the opportunities brought about by these competitions; the prestige of such awards far outweighs their financial value for the fortunate winner. Likewise, Warren has always refused requests to teach or lecture, partly because of her natural reserve, partly because she feels she is not talented in that form of communication; moreover, she has wanted to protect her freedom to compose without interruption, as well as to spend time with her family. To complete an atypical musical profile, Warren has steadfastly refused to establish a base in the East, though most musicians feel this to be professionally necessary. Thus she remains among the few twentieth century composers of international repute whose creative impulses have sprung from and been nurtured in the western United States. However, she acknowledges the importance of the early years spent in New York, where she made musical ties which helped establish the foundations of her career. These decisions to choose a far from traditional course may have left some doors unopened, but they allowed the composer to follow her creative voice in a uniquely independent way. On the whole, her musical output has benefited.

Though there have been honors, and her work well received internationally, there should, perhaps, have been more recognition, given the quality of Warren's output. But it must be remembered that she had been forced to compete in a profession which, at the time she entered it, was largely the domain of males, there being no Women's Movement under whose protective mantle she might have found haven. Moreover, the composer has never been skilled at promoting herself, due to her essentially reserved nature and her belief that she could fulfill her purpose by working single-mindedly at the craft of writing music. However, in this era of "hype" and the media, the creative artist - no matter how talented - must clamor to be heard. Warren has steadfastly resisted seeking publicity or favors from friends in the music field, preferring to let her work speak for her. Her high-mindedness comes through in these comments from a 1966 interview in which she said, "Being financially secure, I follow only my artistic conscience, and never tackle anything to which I feel I can't give my best. A man who must support a family is often forced into areas of composition that are alien to him, and then his time for personal creative satisfaction is limited ... A musical expression should be sincere, and if it is, no matter what the idiom may be, I can accept it. I feel that only sincerity gives the music its chance for survival."

At a time of life when many composers are beginning to limit their output and - to paraphrase Rossini, "pursuing the melodies, rather than being pursued by them" - Elinor was taking on new challenges.

Beginning with her study in Paris with Boulanger, the composer's work had been moving subtly toward a new, more dynamic direction. *Abram in Egypt*, with its urgent, often fierce, and decidedly twentieth century construction, had been the first of her major works to experience the change. In 1970, she accepted another commission, this time from Stanford University, which had enjoyed much success with a recent performance of *Abram*. The university requested an orchestral work to be premiered by their own excellent university symphony orchestra. Warren decided to depart from the standard four-movement symphonic form and create a work which, though contemporary in feeling, would be written in traditional sonata-symphony form, all movements to be contained within the framework of a single movement. Throughout much of the year 1970, she worked on the symphony, completing it shortly before its premiere, December 6 of that year, by the Stanford University Orchestra, Sandor Salgo, conductor.

Symphony in One Movement was later presented to Los Angeles audiences when, in a concert paying tribute to the work of significant contemporary women composers, the Los Angeles Philharmonic performed it May 26, 1972, at Royce Hall, UCLA. The conductor on that occasion was Gerhard Samuel. The sole review of the Los Angeles performance was less enthusiastic than had been newspaper comment on the Stanford premiere, which described "... an outpouring, with a big surging theme through the first section, a smoldering slow movement ... builds up in rising power."

Warren's *Symphony in One Movement* marks an important transition, departing boldly from the neo-Romantic idiom that had been the composer's hallmark. Sophisticated, complex, it is at the same time intellectual and emotional, possessing force and daring that prefigure a new dimension.

The composer has always had a special affinity for orchestral writing, with its great variety of colors; she finds in it "the broader and bigger musical expression which satisfies me." Given the economic realities faced by most orchestras, Warren has been fortunate in the large number of performances her orchestral and choral-orchestral works have received. "It's such a great advantage," she says, "to be able to hear your works performed. Hearing them in your mind is one thing, but when they are performed, you learn the practical side of it - what isn't right and what should be worked over. Often you have a lot of hard work to do after that first performance, but it's worth it. And after hearing many performances of one's works, it is easier to recognize the more subtle possibilities of the instruments."

When writing symphonic music, she carries themes for all the instruments in her head and composes from the "inner ear." Vocal or choral compositions, however, she works out at the piano. She begins first by writing a sketch so as not to lose the flow of the musical idea. There may be only four or five staves in that preliminary sketch, but from that point all else proceeds.

"Then I write and put away," she says, "take a second look and polish; put away again, and finally have it finished. But when I hear one of my compositions later, I sometimes find something I could have done to polish it a little more." For her, orchestrating a work completes the creative process. "One must compose into the orchestration."

A high level of chromaticism and frequent modulations make some of Warren's works difficult to perform. Conductor/musicologist James Fahringer believes that the key to effective performances of Warren's orchestral works is finding the vocal line. "Just as Bach wrote instrumentally, even in his vocal works," says Fahringer, "Elinor Warren is intrinsically a vocal singer, even in her instrumental music."

In 1971, Roger Wagner chose once again to present *The Legend of King Arthur* for his Los Angeles Master Chorale audiences. He believes this work to be one of Warren's finest and its *a cappella* chorus, *More Things Are Wrought By Prayer* to be "a classic by itself." This 1971 performance was the choral symphony's third in Los Angeles; his second as its conductor. It was presented at the Dorothy Chandler Pavilion of the Music Center with the Master Chorale and Sinfonia Orchestra, soloists William Chapman, baritone, and George Metcalfe, a well-known opera tenor from Australia.

Always seeking to view her compositions from a broadened perspective, Elinor had continued to make small alterations in the score of *King Arthur* - subtle changes, but ones she believed to be important. Prior to the performance these were incorporated into the orchestral score and included in a new edition of the work's piano-vocal score, published in 1974, and the first to bear its present title. Following this edition, Warren decided to call the work "completed" - after nearly 35 years.

Though the era of weekly radio concerts by famous concert artists had ended, television ushered in new and larger audiences for classical music; but the amount of serious music heard on the commercial networks was greatly restricted. On September 24, 1962, the Mormon Tabernacle Choir performed *More Things Are Wrought By Prayer* from *The Legend of King Arthur* on their weekly television program. Some years later, August 9, 1981, they performed it again on their weekly broadcast over ABC Radio - one of several of their radio performances of the work.

Quickly upon the *Symphony in One Movement* followed a commission from Occidental College. Warren was urged by colleagues to apply, as well, for a grant from the National Endowment for the Arts to supplement the generous commission. She was awarded the Endowment Fellowship in 1976 and once again chose a Sandburg text for the ensuing composition - her first using narration - *Good Morning, America!* The composer has written of this work:

> For a number of years I had been fascinated with Carl Sandburg's great epic poem. ... The poet had written it in 1927 when he received an honorary degree from Harvard University. I had set others of his poems, but this was in the back of my mind and I kept returning to reading and thinking about it. ... When Occidental College offered me a commission for a major choral-orchestral work, the idea of this particular Sandburg poem again held my imagination, and I set about selecting those portions of the book which seemed to me to express the real nucleus of its power ...

Here once again, as with the *Symphony in One Movement*, Warren paints her musical pictures in a less conventional way. But this work bears a stronger link to her past compositions than does the *Symphony*. There remain, however, indications of a new stylistic path - especially in the orchestration.

Occidental did not premiere *Good Morning, America!*; several years would pass before the college developed an orchestra able to handle such an ambitious undertaking. Instead, Dr. Howard Swan who, for many years had been closely associated with Occidental, gave the first performance of the new work on November 21, 1976, at California State University, Fullerton, with the university's orchestra, its large chorus, and narrator, Roger Ardrey. This was quickly followed, during the Bicentennial year, by a number of performances at other universities.

The work had its first performance with a large professional orchestra and chorus the following year, in December, 1977, by the Honolulu Symphony, Robert LaMarchina conducting. The well-known actor Efrem Zimbalist, Jr. - himself the son of two celebrated musicians - was narrator. For this performance, LaMarchina requested from the composer an augmented brass section to accommodate his very large orchestra. This necessitated a slightly altered windset. Thus, *Good Morning, America!* ended up with both an "A" and a "B" version, though the two orchestrations differ little, except for the added brass parts.

The 1960's and 1970's proved an important period of recognition for the composer's work. During 1976, her songs, *Tawny Days* (from *Singing Earth*) and *Heather* were performed in concert in the nation's capital, at the John F. Kennedy Center for the Performing Arts. That summer, Roger Wagner and his Chorale, with David Jennings as baritone soloist, presented *Abram in Egypt* at the Israel Music Festival. The composer and her husband traveled to Israel for the three performances: August 6 and 7 in Jerusalem; August 8 at Caesarea.

The Caesarea performance was given in the town's 2,000-year-old amphitheatre, built by King Herod. Ruins of Herod's palace could be seen from the stage. After the highly-successful Jerusalem performances, Warren suspected the Caesarea performance might be anticlimactic. It was to prove just the opposite.

That evening, an audience of 5,000 filled the ancient coliseum, built in grand scale like those of Rome. The night offered up a full moon and balmy weather, the Mediterranean gently lapping the nearby shore. Roger Wagner had asked the composer to sit in the front row, so as to be ready to come onstage for bows at the conclusion. Since her husband wished to be further back for better acoustics, Warren sat alone to hear her work performed in the land where Abram and Sarai had lived their story.

Abram in Egypt is a work of many contrasts between dramatic and lyrical moments, proceeding to a conclusion of telling effect, as the full chorus and soloist sing: "Then the Lord said: 'Lift up your eyes, and look from the place where you are/Northward and southward, eastward and westward/Arise, arise and walk! ...'" moving to an ending, broadly sung in striking harmonies of great intensity: ... "'Arise, and walk through the length and breadth of the land, for I will give it to you and your descendants, forever and ever ...'" As these final phrases echoed throughout the amphitheatre, the Israeli concert-goers erupted into cheers, repeatedly bringing onstage the American woman who had given voice to their history. On that night, the setting, weather, performers and audience combined to give the composer what she regards as her most personally memorable musical experience. The day before, at the Shrine of the Book in Jerusalem, she had been treated to a view of the actual papyrus scroll from which she had taken her text.

Earlier, Roger Wagner had recorded *Abram in Egypt* for CRI, conducting the London Philharmonic and his Chorale, featuring as soloist the distinguished British baritone, Ronald Lewis. To date, this and the composer's *Suite for Orchestra*, its companion piece on the disc, remain the only commercially available recordings of any of Warren's major orchestral or choral works; a lamentable loss in view of the repeated assertions of many critics that works such as *The Legend of King*

Arthur and *Requiem* represent a "valuable addition" to the musical literature.

Though involved during these years with creating large, complex works that represented for her a new direction, the composer would take time for travel with her husband, and sometimes her children and grand-children, during a few weeks every summer. She found these experiences renewing and always returned home eager to begin work again. She has composed steadily throughout her life, except for these vacations and respites of two or three weeks following the birth of each of her children. Seeming always to welcome the struggle of creation, she has said, "Music is so elusive. I believe it is the most creative and fascinating of the arts - closely allied with architecture. You can't say how one composes. You really fly-fish. There is a lot of struggle when confronted with a subject such as the *Requiem*. It has to grow and grow. There is a lot of rewrite before it comes out of the shell."

On one of their trips, in September of 1977, Elinor and her husband stopped at Fontainebleau for what was to be the composer's last visit with Nadia Boulanger, who would live only two more years. During sessions of the Conservatoire Américain, Boulanger occupied an apartment on the second floor of the palace, which, Warren notes, was furnished with "her own lovely things." The great teacher had celebrated her 90th birthday two days pre-viously. By now she was in a wheelchair, and students came to the apartment for their lessons. The composer's diary of the trip records that Boulanger looked very frail, but her mind was as acute and perceptive as it had ever been. Being nearly blind, she asked Elinor to sit by a window "in the sunshine" so she would be able to see her faintly. "It was a very touching meeting," wrote Warren, "and even more so at parting."

Shortly after its premiere and a performance in Greece, Warren had felt dissatisfied with her song cycle for soprano or tenor and orchestra, *Singing Earth*. She had withdrawn the composition, putting it away until she could find time to rework it. Not until 1978 did she finally return to it, completely rewriting the orchestration and musical bridges linking the four songs. The work in

its new version was premiered April 29, 1979, at Jordan
Hall, Boston, Antonia Brico conducting the New England
Women's Symphony with Ellen McLain, soprano soloist.
Program notes by the composer for this performance speak
of the changing seasons celebrated in the cycle as
symbolic of succeeding phases of human life, while "the
composition moves to a climax of supplication for nature's
treasures, which enrich all human experience."

During the 1980's, Warren works have been given
noteworthy performances. Her chorus from *The Legend of
King Arthur, More Things Are Wrought By Prayer*, was
presented on January 10, 1980, by the combined choirs of
the Christian College Choral Festival, Dr. Howard Swan
conducting, at Oklahoma's Harding University. On April
21, 1985, Dr. Swan conducted five choirs - 300 voices -
in a performance of the composition at a choral festival
in Des Moines, Iowa. On November 12, 1982, Occidental,
now with a full-sized student orchestra, presented the
choral-orchestral composition the college had commissioned, *Good Morning, America!* The orchestra was
joined by Occidental's Glee Club in a notable performance
of the work. And at Wolf Trap on November 11, 1983, a
group of Warren songs, including *Christmas Candle, For
You With Love*, and *Who Loves the Rain*, were sung by
soprano Lynne Anders.

In January, 1982, Warren was invited to be guest
speaker as part of the UCLA Music Department lecture
series "Women in Music." For this appearance, held at
Schoenberg Hall, the composer made a rare departure
from her reluctance to lecture at universities and schools
of music, discussing her compositions and including
excerpts from recordings of her orchestral and vocal
works.

These years were to bring sad times, as well. Since
the late 1960's, Wayne Griffin had suffered from
Parkinson's disease, as well as other complications.
Nonetheless, he refused to moderate a highly-active life
that continued to involve business and civic leadership, in
addition to almost daily tennis games and weekends at
Rancho Corona del Valle. But in September of 1981, after
a long and valiant struggle with illness, Griffin died at
home, his family by his side.

The year before her husband's death, one of Warren's publishers, Carl Fischer, decided to publish a collection of twelve of her songs and asked the composer to choose those to be included in the volume, *Selected Songs by Elinor Remick Warren.*

At this time music publishers were in the throes of a continuing struggle against the copy machine. Though the unauthorized use of copiers to reproduce copyrighted music is illegal, publishers were finding it less and less practical to print single songs, which could too easily be pirated. The answer to their dilemma seemed to be the song collection. G. Schirmer had already included Warren's *Snow Towards Evening* in their prestigious collection, *Songs by Twenty-Two Americans.* When the composer was still very young, her song *The Heart of a Rose* had been included in a published collection from the repertoire of Margaret Matzenauer; later, *Sweetgrass Range* had been chosen for a collection of Nelson Eddy favorites. *Selected Songs,* however, remains the only collection in print devoted solely to Warren's art songs.

Together, Elinor and Wayne puzzled for months over which of her more than sixty published songs should be included in the Fischer collection. Finally choices were made and the composer went over each composition, in some instances re-editing and providing optional note-changes to accommodate medium-range as well as higher voices. Then she again edited the songs with great care. Ever the perfectionist, Warren continues to polish her compositions until they go to press and sometimes re-edits them for new editions.

Sadly, the first copies of *Selected Songs* reached the composer just months after her husband's death. But the dedication page bore the simple inscription: "To Wayne," as she had told him it would. Theirs had been a remarkable blend of talents, interests and emotions. A knowledgeable and sensitive musician, Griffin is credited by his wife as being an enormous and positive influence on her career. But there was more, touchingly summed up in a letter penned by him to Elinor on an anniversary, over a decade before:

Beloved -

Thirty-four delightful years with you -
each happier than the last - seem like
thirty-four days of a honeymoon. Yet there
are those wonderful children, so it must have
really happened. How about another thirty-
four?

I love you
  "   "   "
  "   "   "
  "   "   "
  "   "   "

Your
Wayne

Now she must continue alone. Always there had been
someone to advise and offer support in her life and
career - first her parents and then her husband. For a
long time, Elinor remained numb with grief and shock.
Finally, however, she resumed piano practice, now beginning each session with her transcription of the Bach air
If Thou Art Near, for it reminded her of her husband.
Occasionally she would appear as accompanist in a program of her songs, and then, slowly, the work began
again. She realized that the profession which had been
hers since the age of five could sustain her even now.

She wrote two works for mixed chorus, *On the
Echoing Green* and *Now Welcome, Summer!*, believing them
to be an interesting pair for performance. They were
accepted for publication in the piano-vocal versions, after
which she also scored them with chamber orchestra
accompaniment. Set to poems by William Blake and
Geoffrey Chaucer, they bear the pure, clear harmonies
that characterize her choral writing.

New demands intruded. Since the early years of her
career, many libraries and universities had been requesting
that she donate her works to their collections. Now she
decided to present manuscripts, letters and scores to the
New York Public Library at Lincoln Center and a complete
collection of all her works to date to the Free Library of
Philadelphia and its Edwin A. Fleisher Collection of
Orchestral Music.

However, many compositions still active in publishers' catalogs and larger works in their rental libraries involved her in much correspondence and musical detail. Added to this were domestic and business responsibilities which must be handled alone. And, as always, there were visits with a devoted family, who maintain a supportive and loving interest in her life and music.

Regardless of other involvements, the composer has continued to find time for sessions at the Steinway she bought so many years ago with earnings from her early professional activities. Her piano chair was her mother's; Elinor had grown up using it. Beside the piano is an ornate 18th century music stand, said to have belonged to a pupil of Mozart. On it, through the years, has always rested Warren's latest published composition.

It is the exceptional quality of her piano that prompted Lance Bowling, of Cambria Records, to suggest to Warren that a recording of her art songs, which he planned, be made in the music room of her home. He and the composer discussed various accompanists, but, after hearing her play, Bowling convinced Warren herself to perform. The subsequent recording, made over a four-day period during June and July of 1986 and released on compact disc as well as cassette tape, is a significant musical document, the composer's active participation providing definitive interpretations of more than two dozen of her vocal works.

Soprano Marie Gibson was Warren's and Bowling's choice for this recording. She possesses an extraordinary range of voice and technique that can easily accommodate the delicate charm of *In A Low Rocking Chair* or the long, powerful phrases of *White Horses of the Sea*. Flutist Catherine Smith joined Gibson and Warren on five of the songs for which the composer had written special flute obbligatos.

Warren, who had not made a recording since the series of piano accompaniments in the 1930's, was fascinated by the technical aspects of the experience. She and the production staff were delighted by the acoustical qualities of her music room. The only problems were created by sounds from an occasional lawn-mower or passing truck which, no matter how faint, could be picked up by the sensitive digital equipment. Because the songs were recorded also for compact disc release, sound conditions had to be perfect. Musicians and technicians worked long hours and recorded many "takes" to achieve a result not only of historic importance but of artistic merit.

It is in this downstairs music room where the composer prefers to work during the sensitive early stages of creating a composition. Here she can close herself behind heavy wood doors and feel complete solitude. At one end of the large, high-ceilinged room is her concert grand; along one side, large glass doors opening onto the garden. In this setting, she can experience the "aloneness" she needs for concentrated work. Warren has always preferred working with windows and doors closed, giving her the sense of being totally isolated.

Much of the later stage of work on a composition is done in the composer's upstairs studio, where she can spread out her manuscript pages and they will remain undisturbed from day to day. This room is a contrast to the rest of the comfortably appointed house. It is spartan, simply furnished; obviously a place where a great deal of no-nonsense activity takes place. Large windows look onto a green expanse of lawn, flower borders and trees. On the walls are the room's only purely decorative elements - a small painting of water-lilies presented to her by an artist friend in tribute to her song *If You Have Forgotten*; a color print reminiscent of her song *White Horses of the Sea*; a print of the drawing done by Chagall for Nadia Boulanger's eightieth birthday celebration. Against one wall is a blonde wood spinet piano; beside it the large draftsman's board given her by Wayne for work on her scores. There is about the room a sense of peace and introspection which reflect the nature of its occupant, who once revealed, in an interview for the *Christian Science Monitor*, the philosophy governing her accomplishment:

> I'm fully aware of the demands of the art, but I believe with Schweitzer that being a fine musician isn't enough. You should strive to be a fine human being, too.

> If I hadn't married and had a family, I would naturally have had much more time to devote to music, but certainly I'm a far richer, happier person for having taken the path I did.

Besides new recordings of Warren's music, there are more compositions in progress and many performances to come. Three decades after its premiere, her *Suite for Orchestra* continues to impress critics, the *Baltimore Evening Sun* writing, following a 1986 performance, "The crown of the concert was this pure, delightful impressionism by one of America's truly fine composers." And on a recent birthday, Los Angeles's classical music station, KFAC, singled her out for congratulations throughout its broadcast day.

It is apparent that Elinor Remick Warren remains close to the world she chose at the age of five. In a profession still largely dominated by men, she has transcended the prejudice toward women without surrendering her womanhood. Above all, with heart and craft, she has defended her musical ideas, maintained her own voice.

Significantly, Warren remains one of very few women composers of international repute to focus on the creation of large works for chorus and full orchestra. Of her art, she has simply said, "I have always tried to write music as I feel it." It may be many years before the lasting values of her music can be accurately assessed. A more conservative trend seems imminent. But there remains something intangible, something beyond a trend or a moment. It lies in great ideas, and in the heart of the listener.

Perhaps a clue to the future might be gleaned from a comment by Roger Wagner at the reception following his 1971 performance of her *Legend of King Arthur*. Observing the five-foot composer greeting well-wishers, Wagner toasted her: "Such a little lady - such gigantic thoughts."

CHRONOLOGY OF
MAJOR ORCHESTRAL AND CHORAL WORKS

Works are listed by date of completion or major revision. For dates of copyrights and premieres, see the Catalog of Works (p. 155).

1932	*The Harp Weaver*
1940	*The Passing of King Arthur*
1946	*The Crystal Lake*
1951	*The Sleeping Beauty*
1951	*Singing Earth*
1954	*Suite for Orchestra*
1954	*Along the Western Shore*
1954	*Sonnets for Soprano and String Quartet/ String Orchestra*
1958	*Transcontinental*
1959	*Abram in Egypt*
1960	*Revision: Suite for Orchestra*
1965	*Requiem*
1970	*Symphony in One Movement*
1974	Revision: *The Passing of King Arthur* (retitled *The Legend of King Arthur*)
1976	*Good Morning, America!*
1978	Revision: *Singing Earth*

MUSICAL STYLE AND PRINCIPAL WORKS

Elinor Warren's career as a composer may be divided into three eras. The first of these is distinguished by the forms in which she worked, the latter by an evolution in style. Her early period extends from approximately 1922 through the years spent touring as assisting artist with a number of distinguished singers and up to the 1936 New York premiere of the orchestral version of *The Harp Weaver*. During this time she wrote art songs and smaller choral works, *a cappella* or with piano or organ accompaniment, as well as several compositions for piano. During the middle years of her career she began to write for orchestra. This period includes a number of larger works for orchestra and some of her most important works for orchestra with chorus. The latter period of Warren's career, when stylistic changes in her characteristic neo-Romanticism become evident, can be said to date from the 1950's. It was then that she spent several months in private study with Nadia Boulanger. This began a long and close friendship with Boulanger that was to be a distinct influence on the composer's later major works.

Though the early period of Warren's career produced numerous art songs and smaller choral compositions, she has continued writing in these forms throughout her life. The songs are characterized by stylistic variation and a notable melding of text and music. Warren has tried from her earliest years as a composer to create an atmosphere about her songs; a meaning beyond what words alone can convey. Concerned that the listener to a song be able to understand its words upon first hearing, she is always conscious of vocal ranges and demands, so as to make possible proper projection of the words.

A subtle introspection marks many of the finest of these songs. *Snow Towards Evening* captures in its somber opening chords the gray stillness of snow falling as night looms. A lyrical, rising vocal line sets the mood of the song over a gentle, flowing accompaniment [Example 1]. At the song's conclusion tenderly descending phrases for both voice and accompaniment settle all into peaceful quietude.

The Nights Remember begins gently, poignantly, with a pattern of enharmonic changes in its accompaniment during the first six measures, followed by tonic harmonies. The song becomes joyous and animated at its center, then ends again in introspective, wistful phrases [Example 2].

If You Have Forgotten opens with an accompaniment that reflects the undulating movement of the "floating water lilies" of Sara Teasdale's poem [Example 3]. After a *poco agitato* middle section, the song returns to the emotion of the melodic opening passages. This time, however, it is shadowed by the sadness inherent in the preceding measures.

Piano, whose text is an unusual poem by D.H. Lawrence, expresses from the first a wistfulness and poignancy in its flowing phrases and in the harmonic changes employed [Example 4]. Its middle section, musically, is fraught with the poem's drama. The song ends with a repetition of its opening measures, as the music resumes its wistful opening mood, though now in an extended line.

Lonely Roads, with words by John Masefield, opens with a pattern of octaves in the lower bass accompaniment reflective of the rhythm of walking [Example 5]. This is then contrasted by a flowing, warmly melodic section. As the song develops there is always a feeling of poignancy - even in the more dramatic middle section. This introspective mood predominates at the end, as the song closes with the same octave pattern in the bass that appeared at the beginning.

In direct contrast to these mood songs are others, like *White Horses of the Sea,* and the later *We Two* and *Heather,* which exhibit a forward propulsion, moving with joyous abandon to powerful endings. In these songs and others like them the accompaniments are highly pianistic - even orchestral - accompanist and singer performing as full partners in expressing the text.

From its strong opening measures, *White Horses of the Sea* is a song in which voice and piano are of equal importance, as the plunging ocean waves - described in chords and arpeggios of 16th notes - are likened to "great white horses." After a calmer melodic middle section the piano resumes the earlier forward thrust [Example 6] and a dramatic climax is reached in both voice and piano.

Another song of this type is the exultant *We Two*. Beginning with strong, full A major chords in the accompaniment, under long-held forte notes in the vocal line, it is indeed a composition for both voice and piano [Example 7]. Even in the song's more lyrical and quiet middle section, there is always the feeling of forward, driving momentum. Eventually this builds to a jubilant close.

In the song *Heather*, the rhythmic, flowing movement of purple heather on the Scottish highlands and moors is suggested from the opening measures [Example 8] and continues throughout the song. This gradually builds to a joyous closing section which climaxes as the voice sustains a long-held tonic G above the staff over sweeping, upward arpeggios in the piano.

Though her catalog of published art songs to date numbers sixty-five, Warren has written an even greater number of choral compositions for various combinations of voices, *a cappella*, and with piano or organ accompaniment. These works, both secular and religious, are characterized by deft rhythmic and stylistic invention. Warren regards the choral writing of her early career as being an important step in moving her toward the larger dimension of orchestral writing that came during the middle period of her career. When this occurred, she nonetheless continued, as she does today, composing choral songs.

Two of her most recent compositions in this genre are set to poems by English writers: *Now Welcome, Summer!* by Geoffrey Chaucer and *On the Echoing Green* by William Blake. Musically, they are contemporary in style, especially in the accompaniments. Yet they retain a traditionalism appropriate to their 14th and 18th century texts. Composed for SATB, these choral songs program well together, though not written as a pair and published separately [Examples 9 and 10].

Of particular interest for choirs is the set of seven introits, prayer responses, and benedictions for SATB titled *Praises and Prayers*. They have been ingeniously composed to allow performance equally effectively *a cappella*, with organ accompaniment, or with the addition of two trumpets and two trombones. The little collection includes jubilant introits for Christmas [Example 11] and Easter [Example 12].

Three songs grouped together for SSA are published with the title *Little Choral Suite*. The first, *Rain Slippers*, gives the impression of raindrops in its staccato piano accompaniment [Example 13]. The second, *Sleep Walks Over the Hill*, with its slow, gently swinging rhythm, has the quality of a lullaby [Example 14]. The third, *A Little Song of Life*, projects an affirmative mood of happy assurance [Example 15]. Though any one of these songs may be sung separately, they are usually performed as a short cycle.

Another song for SSA and piano is *White Iris*. Its text by Bliss Carman tells of an ancient princess for whom the flower supposedly was named. The song's modal qualities reflect a mood of mystery and the beauty experienced in a remote garden of white irises [Example 16].

My Heart is Ready, marked *moderato giocoso*, has as its text words from the 108th Psalm. It is set for SATB voices and organ. A rhythmic, syncopated pattern affirms joyous assurance [Example 17] as the song moves toward a climax of praise and thankfulness.

The Night Will Never Stay, for SSA voices with piano, is set to a wistful poem by Eleanor Farjeon. In mood it resembles many of Warren's introspective songs for solo voice, ending with a questioning musical phrase as each voice part echoes the poem's elusive feeling: "The night will never stay, The night will slip away." The song itself seems to "slip away," as it concludes in harmonies of the minor subdominant 11th [Example 18].

During the middle era of Warren's career, extending from the premiere of the choral-orchestral version of *The Harp Weaver* in 1936, to *Along the Western Shore* in 1955, the composer now writes for full orchestra in a number of major compositions. Though still at home in the

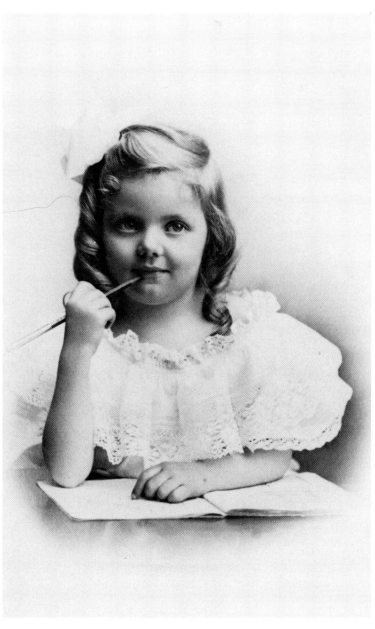

Elinor Remick Warren on the eve of
her fifth birthday and her first music lesson.
This photograph was suggested by her grandmother
"so you will always remember this event."

Elinor at her mother's piano, following her first major appearance as a pianist, age 8. She played a Mozart sonata for two pianos with celebrated pianist Thilo Becker.

On the porch of her house at 9th and Alvarado Streets, at about age 10, holding the doll "Kate," given her by her music teacher, Kathryn Montreville Cocke.

Maude Remick and James Garfield Warren,
the composer's parents,
at the time of their marriage in 1895.

For a brief period during and just after high school, Elinor added the harp to her musical accomplishments. For several programs with singers she played a group of accompaniments on the instrument, which proved to be popular with audiences.

While studying with Frank LaForge in New York, the young composer/pianist is pictured with Metropolitan Opera star Margaret Matzenauer, with whom she toured as assisting artist, and Harold Flammer, one of her early publishers.

With British conductor Albert Coates,
following the world premiere of her choral symphony,
The Passing [Legend] of King Arthur, 1940.

Elinor Warren with her husband,
producer and business leader Z. Wayne Griffin.

The Griffins with their three children -
a family Christmas card, 1941.
Son Jim is to the far left;
Elayne on her mother's lap;
Wayne, Jr., seated on the piano.

The Hancock Park house where the composer raised her
family and where she lives and works today.

Warren after receiving her honorary Doctor of Music
degree from Occidental College, 1954.
To the left is Dr. Raymond Kendall, Dean of the
School of Music, University of Southern California;
to the right, Dr. Howard Swan, whose Occidental
College choirs have presented most of her choral works.

Conductor Roger Wagner confers with the composer in her
music room preparing for his 1966 premiere performance
of *Requiem*, which he commissioned.

Taking a bow, along with baritone Paul Hinshaw and
soprano Carol Neblett, following the world premiere of
Requiem, presented by Roger Wagner and the Los Angeles
Master Chorale and Sinfonia Orchestra at the Dorothy
Chandler Pavilion of the Los Angeles Music Center.

With Andre Kostelanetz at a rehearsal of the Minnesota Orchestra which he conducted October 31, 1975 at Minneapolis, playing *The Crystal Lake* with the composer in the audience.

Greeting her teacher and close friend Nadia Boulanger at
Boulanger's surprise eightieth birthday celebration
in Monaco, September 30, 1967.

Roger Wagner introduces Warren
to members of the orchestra during a rehearsal for a
series of performances of *Abram in Egypt*, presented in
Jerusalem and Caesarea at the Israel Music Festival, 1976.

With actor Efrem Zimbalist, Jr., rehearsing for the Honolulu performance of her Bicentennial work for mixed chorus, narrator and orchestra, *Good Morning, America!*

The composer introduces four of her grandchildren to her *Songs for Young Voices,* which is dedicated to them.

Elinor and Wayne Griffin are joined by children and grandchildren for a family Christmas portrait, 1980.

astringent realms of the art song, Warren at this period finds herself equally attracted to ample orchestrations. Yet even here she acknowledges the debt she owes to the former: "The singers have influenced me a lot. I like to make each instrument sing." Conductor/musicologist James Fahringer claims that the way to study Warren's often complex orchestral scores is to look for the underlying melodic lines; he feels she tends to think vocally, no matter what the form.

The composer, drawn toward introspection in her personal life, seems to be especially touched by beauty in solitude, whether the stirring majesty of great cloud patterns above a sun-drenched desert as in *Suite for Orchestra*, or the haunting, wistful landscape of *Along the Western Shore*'s second movement. In these works, lacking words to consider, Warren does not attempt to express in music a picture so much as to express a feeling or the emotions evoked by a scene. Therefore, the often-played tone poem, *The Crystal Lake*, does not portray in music the description of the scene. Rather, it recreates the emotions awakened in the composer by her discovery of the lake - an experience which moved her so deeply it could find its natural expression only in music. A work of American impressionism, *The Crystal Lake* is scored for woodwinds in pairs, brass, strings, harp and percussion. At its beginning, the eerie, remote characteristics of the scene are expressed by woodwinds and by *tremolo* strings in the high registers [Example 19]. Soon the horns are heard and as the drama of nature and its changing elements is expressed, the full orchestra enters with strong rhythms and vigorous movement. An extended middle section features *divisi* strings and woodwinds in increasing agitation until finally they are overcome with the return of the first themes [Example 20]. Again the music takes on the former quality of serenity, finishing as it began, in a mood of enduring peacefulness.

Throughout her career, the composer would seem to have preferred the full tonal range of the symphony orchestra to the more restricted colors of the chamber ensemble. This is clearly evident in *Along the Western Shore*, inspired by lines from the poetry of three American poets: Edward Arlington Robinson, Robert Nathan, and Walt Whitman.

The work's first movement opens in a somber mood, progressing with rich harmonies through passages of growing intensity that culminate in a fervid song for full orchestra. This first theme [Example 21] is repeated in the low strings and brass, while over it muted horns and woodwinds, with high strings tremolo, lend a mystic quality in bringing the movement to a close.

Next follows a nocturne, or night song, its tender melody [Example 22], first sung by the English horn, later by solo viola and finally by the violins and brass. After building to a climax of warmth and breadth, the movement gradually comes to a close with slowly fading harmonies.

The work's third movement expresses the restlessness of the sea, its surging waves breaking against a shore [Example 23]. Even in quieter moments there is felt an undercurrent of urgency. A mysterious mood begins at measure 38 and builds in excitement toward the return of the first theme. This is now heard in a major key, leading, through use of the brasses, to a triumphant close.

Also during the middle years of Warren's career appear large compositions for chorus and soloists with orchestra, such as *The Harp Weaver* (1932), *The Legend of King Arthur* (1940), *The Sleeping Beauty* (1951) and *Transcontinental* (1958). As with many of the songs and smaller choruses she continued to compose during this period, the most significant of these works are expressive of a deeply-rooted spiritual outlook.

In her earliest orchestral compositions, especially the impressionistic *Crystal Lake* and a shorter work, *The Fountain*, the composer features the harp. This is also to be observed in the first of Warren's large works, her first with full orchestra, *The Harp Weaver*.

A musical blend of the composer's essential traditionalism and her use of more contemporary musical idioms mirror the text by Edna St. Vincent Millay, which utilizes an Irish legend to symbolize deeper and more complex ideas. The pure voices of a women's chorus add to the other-worldliness of the overall composition.

Musical unity is achieved by use of a poignant, folk-like motive, repeated at intervals throughout the composition and first heard in the flute over harp accompaniment [Example 24].

The work opens with the baritone soloist's narrative, soon continued and enlarged by the chorus. There is a close interplay between chorus and baritone, as the story is recounted by the chorus, and the baritone reflects upon the spiritual fantasy that is unfolding. In keeping with the text, a harp is featured in the orchestration. For the piano-vocal version, effectively given in many performances here and abroad, the harp becomes an optionally added soloist. Words and music intimately merge in the strongly melodic passages that flow gently from section to section, and rise at last to a peak of spiritual triumph [Example 25].

Four years after the New York premiere for full orchestra of *The Harp Weaver* came the world premiere of *The Legend of King Arthur*, then titled *The Passing of King Arthur*. With this composition, one of Warren's most significant, the composer exhibits a pure idealism as she seems to stand apart from the world, observing it through a mystic lens. Though at a later period mystical subject-matter is again addressed by Warren in her *Requiem*, she is by then expressing herself in more bold, passionate musical terms. During these middle years the composer views the world from a stance that is positive, idealistic, concerned primarily with life's beauty and goodness. However, some of her art songs of this period reflect a mood quite different; one of sadness and loneliness. This may be attributed in part to the nature of their texts, but more so to the composer's ability to reproduce an emotion or recreate a scene through the more abstract musical form.

The Legend of King Arthur continues a long-established tradition of choral writing that reached its apogee in England and to a lesser degree found its place in American music as well. This choral symphony for orchestra with mixed chorus and soloists is based on Alfred Tennyson's narrative poem *The Passing of Arthur*, from his classic work *Idylls of the King*. It portrays the last hours of the legendary English ruler. Warren's composition stresses not only the drama of the king's story but also its developing spiritual qualities.

The work is constructed in two large sections, separated by the orchestral *Intermezzo*, which links the dramatic first portion to the more spiritual second. The composer uses chorus and soloists virtually as the actors and chorus were used in ancient Greek drama; the chorus to narrate events to the audience and the soloists (in this case, baritone and tenor) to portray principal characters in the drama.

Unity is achieved through use of certain identifying motives that recur throughout. The following examples are taken from the first appearances of major motives in the piano-vocal score. Some of them are heard a number of times: *The King Arthur Theme* [Example 26]; *Excalibur* [Example 27] - this motive is heard more often than any other; *Lake Waters* [Example 28]; and *The Barge* [Example 29].

As the drama of Part I unfolds, there are vivid contrasts in the music which show strength and boldness, along with much that is reflective, mysterious, tender and lyrical. After this highly dramatic first section comes the *Intermezzo*. Besides dividing the two parts, it serves to prepare the listener for the mood to follow. The *Intermezzo* is written in song form, ABA, and features a poignant melody in E minor, first played by the bass clarinet [Example 30]. The middle section begins in the relative key of G major [Example 31] with rich chords in strings and woodwinds, their rhythmic pulsation accenting the fourth count of each measure. After enharmonic changes into other keys, the original melody in E minor for the bass clarinet returns, this time with greater fullness and added support from the whole orchestra. The climax, with forte brass, is echoed softly by strings and woodwinds. In conclusion, a few measures are played even more softly, as four violins echo the opening phrase of the middle section, now in a minor key.

Part II emphasizes the more spiritual side of the work, but always there is an undercurrent of tension as the ancient legend unfolds. This tension is consistently heightened by the music, which contrasts the poignant

sadness of the last hours of the king's life with the fulfillment of his final command, that Excalibur be returned
to the lake from which it came. *King Arthur's Farewell*,
an aria sung by the baritone in one of the work's most
important sections [Example 32] is also published separately, as is the *a cappella* chorus, *More Things Are
Wrought By Prayer*, an extension of the *King Arthur's
Farewell* theme.

As the work draws toward its close there is an ever-
rising building by orchestra and chorus. First comes a
fugue, begun by tenors and baritones, then joined by the
full chorus and orchestra with increasing intensity. As the
music continues building to its striking conclusion, the
chorus proclaims, "For so the whole round earth is every
way bound by gold chains about the feet of God!" and
there is triple forte support by the full orchestra under
the long-held last chords in A major.

Two compositions written during this middle period
presage the more contemporary direction in which Warren
would move in the latter phase of her career. These are
Sonnets for Soprano and String Quartet/String Orchestra
and *Transcontinental.*

The song cycle *Sonnets for Soprano and String
Quartet/String Orchestra* is set to poems from Edna St.
Vincent Millay's *Fatal Interview*, a work considered by
many critics to be among Millay's most contemporary, due
to its existential tone. Because of the intimate character
of the poems, the composer considered them to be
particularly well suited for string quartet with voice.
However she later also arranged the work for string
orchestra, adding double bass and making other adjust-
ments in the strings.

From Millay's collection of fifty-two sonnets, Warren
chose four; one from each phase of the relationship about
which the poet writes. The work opens (Sonnet 7) with
music of intensity and great agitation in the strings; the
soprano does not enter until the 15th measure. Her opening phrase in a dramatic forte passage is repeated by the
strings at the song's climax [Example 33].

After a few measures for the strings in a calmer
mood, both music and words take on a tone of introspec-

tion [Example 34]. The second song (Sonnet 11) is warm and melodic, with an undercurrent of poignancy in its expressive phrases.

This mood is felt even more in the third song, with an added element of deep foreboding and questioning in phrases of a reflective nature.

The fourth song of the cycle (Sonnet 52) is one of final resignation and tranquility, but through its melodic passages one perceives echoes of the tragic past.

Transcontinental, with text by A.M. Sullivan, takes listeners on a journey by train across the United States. It is written for orchestra and chorus SATB, with baritone soloist. Though its subject matter is of a lighter nature than many of Warren's works, it is vital and rich in rhythmic and harmonic variation. There is a distinctly contemporary expression to the music as it paints the vivid contrasts of the poem. While this is particularly apparent in the version with orchestra, the piano-vocal score has a very pianistic accompaniment which is equally effective [Example 35].

In 1959, Warren went to Paris, where she spent three months in intensive study with the renowned musical pedagogue, Nadia Boulanger. The two worked six days each week, in private sessions. A close friendship developed from this association which continued to the end of Boulanger's life, lending further direction to Warren's musical output.

The composer recalls that during her sessions with Boulanger she was drawn toward opening up her style in a more contemporary direction. The influence of this period expressed itself from then on in her work. However, Warren's style had already been evolving toward the more mature expression of this latter period of her career, as can be seen in *Sonnets for Soprano and String Quartet* (1954) and in *Transcontinental* (1958). Her *Suite for Orchestra* and song cycle *Singing Earth* had both also been written prior to the Paris sessions. But the important changes apparent in their revisions - made after that time - put them stylistically with works of the composer's latter career.

Suite for Orchestra, written in 1955, revised in 1960, offers new dimensions to Warren's work. Inspired by characteristic cloud patterns that could be seen from her mountain ranch, the composer now frees herself from all stylistic constraints to create earthy, passionate music; music that, nonetheless, continues to reveal skilled craftsmanship.

The *Suite's* first movement, titled *Black Cloud Horses*, is from the beginning *allegro agitato*, as expressed by strings building, with added brass and followed by woodwinds, to the first theme at measures 10 and 11 [Example 36]. This theme is developed at length, painted in stormy, tumultuous orchestral colors punctuated by *pizzicato* strings. The rhythmic second theme [Example 37] is introduced by the brass in B-flat minor. This second theme is then joined by the full orchestra, moving with driving intensity into other keys and rhythms, finally returning to the first theme. The movement ends with a long, rising crescendo of strings and woodwinds in chromatic fourths over sustained brass to its *fortissimo* close in G minor.

The work's second movement, *Cloud Peaks* (*andante molto tranquillo*) offers surging melodic lines introduced by flutes and clarinets over an accompaniment of harp and soft strings. The opening song-like first theme is followed by a gentle but spritely section heard first in the violas in measure 26, afterwards tossed from one instrument to another but always over a mystical, rich background. Another song-like theme is introduced by the cellos and basses in octaves [Example 38] and later heard in other instrumentations and inversions. An impressionistic, introspective mood prevails overall but soars to triumphal heights before settling to a reflective close.

The *scherzino allegretto* third movement, *Ballet of the Midsummer Sky*, presents a contrasting light, witty interplay between woodwinds and strings, with delicate touches of brass and percussion [Example 39]. There are several departures into other keys and developing themes, one of which is first heard at measure 72-75 [Example 40] and repeated a number of times. Other little themes dart in and out of the tone picture until the return of the opening theme, which moves to a conclusion of joyous abandon.

The final movement, *moderato,* entitled *Pageant Across the Sky,* is a stately processional, beginning *pianissimo* as if coming from afar. The *pizzicato* figure in lower bass strings over which the first theme is heard [Example 41] continues through twenty-one measures. The opening bass figure continues repeatedly, as does the first theme, developed in various instruments and ranges, always plunging forward with rising strength, heightened by the brass and percussion. Over the first theme in the bass registers is heard a new theme of triumph in the upper registers [Example 42] that mounts to the *Suite*'s exultant conclusion.

Prior to her sessions with Nadia Boulanger, Warren was commissioned to write a composition based on the Biblical story of Abram and Sarai as recounted in the Dead Sea Scrolls. She arrived in France with a manuscript in rough draft and spent some of the time with Boulanger discussing the work. A new direction is evident in the completed cantata, *Abram in Egypt.*

For her text, Warren used not only the story as told in a book of the Dead Sea Scrolls, the Genesis Apocryphon (Columns XIX and XX), but portions recounted as well in the Book of Genesis (XII:10-20, XIII:14). The weaving together of these two sources by the composer combines the more detailed and poetic account of the Scrolls with the briefer, more factual and straightforward narrative from Genesis. Warren's feeling for place and tradition removes the listener musically to the ancient world of Abram and Sarai; however the cantata exhibits, as well, a stylistic freedom that is contemporary.

An orchestral introduction sets the mood for the story that follows, which is sung by the chorus, entering with men's voices at the 60th measure and joined four measures later by women's voices [Example 43]. This is the pattern throughout the work - the chorus acting as commentator, and the baritone soloist singing the words of Abram. Only through use of the chorus and the extended solos by Abram does the listener feel - almost see - the presence of Sarai, about whom the story hinges. The baritone's first solo gives a sense of the drama that follows. In this section, the chorus is heard only briefly to provide musical background and take up the progress of the story.

Soon follows another, very melodic solo by Abram, a lyrical paeon of praise and love for Sarai [Example 44]. This is accompanied in the orchestra chiefly by harp and *pizzicato* strings, while the chorus intensifies the emotion with obbligato-like phrases.

As the story unfolds there follows still another solo sung by the baritone; the chorus, treated as added instrumentation, joins with the orchestra. Developing the excitement of the text, chorus and soloist with ever greater intensity each take part in the building of the work, musically and dramatically. Here a forward momentum is established which powerfully carries the listener to a massive climax as chorus and orchestra move to a positive, affirmative ending on a triumphant forte final tonic triad [Example 45].

During this latter portion of her career, Warren returns to the spiritual purity and idealism of earlier works with *Requiem*, commissioned by Roger Wagner and premiered by the Los Angeles Master Chorale and Sinfonia Orchestra, conducted by Wagner, in 1966. Here, however, the musical statement shows the development that has occurred over more than twenty-five years. Climaxes are more subtle, refined, the mysticism less remote than in the composer's 1940 choral symphony, *The Legend of King Arthur*.

Requiem is characterized by contrasts in the employment of vocal and orchestral timbres, in *tempi* and dynamics. The first section, the *Introit*, in the key of G minor, opens with brief introductory measures in the strings and woodwinds. At the seventh measure, low strings in *pizzicato* octaves are heard, which rhythmic pattern occurs throughout the *Introit* and *Kyrie* and again at the conclusion of the entire work. The chorus enters *pianissimo* at the 8th measure, in a prayer for all who have died - a prayer of faith in eternal life. This builds to a fervid hymn of praise, followed at once by the *Kyrie*, in 6/4 time, sung (optionally) *a cappella* [Example 46]. This prayer for God's mercy and eternal peace closes on the minor dominant, ending the first section.

The *Graduale* begins with an introduction by the English horn and violas; then the chorus enters singing a phrase in the manner of an ancient Gregorian chant. This leads to a broad climax, the chorus voicing the conviction that those who live a righteous life on earth will be remembered eternally and have life everlasting. The orchestra closes this section as it began, with the same theme by the English horn and violas and a counter-theme from the opening measures repeated in lower bass octaves [Example 47].

The *Dies Irae* is the work's longest movement, written in through-compositional style rather than as a series of separate sections. It offers a distinct contrast to the rest of the composition, beginning in an ominous, mysterious atmosphere, followed by a *crescendo agitato* when the chorus enters with a strong theme heard repeatedly throughout the entire movement [Example 48]. This portion of the work pictures the Day of Judgment, with passages of dark foreboding in the orchestra. The baritone and then the soprano soloist are heard singing of these moments of insecurity and appealing to a merciful God. The soprano's solo [Example 49] in this slowly rising, questioning section, begins in the lower vocal register, is echoed at the third measure (measure 147) by the flute and joined in the next measure by a solo viola. Together, the three soloists sing questioning phrases; this section closes with their unresolved doubts. This is followed, however, with an outburst of assurance by the chorus ("*Rex Traemendae!*") proclaiming the King of Glory. The *Dies Irae* continues in a more reflective mood of calm as the chorus, then the baritone soloist, sing a plea for mercy. This is followed by a tender, almost child-like melody sung *a cappella*, after which the segment closes in a mood of tranquil assurance.

The *Offertorium: Dominae Jesu Christe* begins and ends with a flowing phrase for the English horn that is the main theme [Example 50]. Use of the English horn is one of the composer's favorite devices, when that colorful palette is appropriate. Again are voiced the insecurities and forebodings of the *Dies Irae* section, accentuated by broken rhythms in the orchestra. But once again, the assurance of salvation is proclaimed, now by the soprano joining the chorus.

The baritone soloist is heard in the *Hostias* with prayers of joyful assurance for all who have passed from earth to everlasting life. The chorus extends this theme, remembering God's promise to all the faithful.

Following is the *Sanctus* section, portraying serene joy and building to exultant praise. Here there is no uncertainty. The chorus (often in eight parts) and soloists join in a dialogue declaring God's glory. They combine with the orchestra to proclaim "Glory be Thine!" There follows the first singing of the *Hosanna*, with its spritely rhythms of happiness [Example 51]. Then at the introduction of the *Benedictus* the mood changes to one of deep spirituality, with the baritone soloist and the men's chorus heard in measures of calm assurance. Finally, the lively *Hosanna* is repeated by the full chorus, ending the movement on a jubilant climax.

There follows the *Agnus Dei*, beginning with a tranquil, flowing melody for chorus, with accompaniment in soft strings. After a short contrapuntal developmental section there is a return to the first poignant melody, sung *a cappella* by the chorus, later joined by the orchestra in a final prayer. The last section of the work is the *Lux Aeterna*, in which the soprano soloist first sings a message of faith which is then reiterated by a chorus of women's voices over a soft accompaniment. They are later joined by the full chorus, as the doctrine of an all-forgiving, all-loving God is repeated.

Now there is a return to the music of the work's opening section (the *Introit*) as the chorus offers a final prayer [Example 52]. The chorus sings the last "amens" to an accompaniment of sustained chords in muted brass and strings over the G minor pedal point in the lower bass instruments as heard at the beginning. The *Requiem* concludes in a mood of utter serenity, which seems to carry the music on and beyond hearing.

In works written during the decade of the 1970's, Warren reaches a new dimension. No longer does neo-Romanticism predominate; it is joined by a more refined intellectualism.

With *Symphony in One Movement* (1970), the composer's innate lyricism now appears as in a dream; the
dream frequently overtaken by clash and agitation. Though
written in symphonic form, its three movements flow from
one to the next without pause, within the framework of a
single movement. Sophisticated, complex, the work combines emotion and intellect in a contemporary idiom.

The first movement begins with a tenuous, questioning
phrase, first in the lower strings and woodwinds, continued by clarinets with oboes, followed by the flutes,
with *pizzicato* strings sharpening the rising, questioning
phrases. The full orchestra then states the vigorous,
decisive first theme [Example 53]. This is developed and
accented singly by various instruments in a variety of
ways in both fragmentary and extended phrases of wide
contrast. These questioning and answering phrases lead
into counter-themes, with much interplay of strings,
woodwinds, brass and percussion, but always with a strong
driving force and often echoing the first themes that are
repeated many times in various ways. These active, often
driving phrases gradually become tranquil in soft strings
with *pianissimo* brass of French horns and trombones.

There follows the *Andante* movement - reflective,
wistful and peaceful overall, though an interruption of
more activity cuts into the pervading tranquility, as if
one must not dream too long. After this restless section,
the former peaceful mood returns. This is followed by the
most lyrical section of the work. It is like a little song,
first heard in the flutes and oboe, later joined by
clarinets and soft strings - a flowing, gentle melody in
spite of its frequent changes of time, alternating from
6/8 to 5/8 to 3/8 [Example 54]. At its gentle close, the
restless, driving spirit is again resumed. This continues
throughout the *con brio* final movement in rondo form.
Beginning with measures 306-308, Violins I [Example 55],
there is a continuing forward drive. No tenuous questioning or restlessness here, but a confident, joyous declara-
tion building to a strong E major finale.

In addition to frequent changes of tempo, Warren
often adds richness to her songs and many of her orchestral compositions through use of key changes, as she has
done in her song cycle for soprano or tenor with orches-

tra, *Singing Earth*. Though essentially written in 1951, during the 1970's this work underwent extensive reworking of its orchestration and, for this reason as well as overall style and musical content, rightfully belongs in Warren's later period.

Like the earlier *Suite for Orchestra*, *Singing Earth* paints its emotions in vivid, passionate hues. But the bold harmonies and angular melodic lines relate in spirit to this later period. Again set to Sandburg poems, the soaring, sustained vocal passages of this cycle are supported by some of the composer's richest and fullest orchestral writing. Dissatisfied with her earlier vision of the work, Warren now shortened the orchestral bridges between songs, strengthened and tightened her orchestration where she felt it to be appropriate, and made some changes in the instrumentation.

After an orchestral introduction with thematic material from the English horn, *The Wind Sings Welcome* is introduced by the voice. Voice and orchestra play back and forth, joining forces in an exuberant phrase, "Have you ever seen such flicking heels before/Silver jig heels on a purple sky rim?" [Example 56] before soaring to a triumphant conclusion at the words "Come along always, come along now!"

Following an orchestral interlude which echoes a motive from the last section and then moves into the tranquil strains of *Summer Stars*, the voice begins a gentle melodic line that sings of the mystery and eternity of a summer sky. One sees Sandburg's "sky bowl" reflected in this music; the nearness of stars in the summer sky. The reflective concluding phrases, "Bend low, bend low again, night of summer stars," are reflective of the opening measures of the song and mirror the subtle magic of a warm summer evening [Example 57].

Out of this tranquil feeling stirs a restlessness in the orchestra, leading to *Tawny Days* which presents an entirely different mood. This is the only song of the cycle whose text deals with emotion in a personal manner. In urgent, strong crescendos contrasted with phrases of subtle delicacy an autumnal mood is evoked. Orchestra and voice build to a forte climax, then decrescendo to an introspective, extended phrase at the concluding words, "Tawny days: and your face again." [Example 58]

Now the orchestra gathers force in the strings, moving with turbulence toward an explosion of sound and emotion in the cycle's final section, *Great Memories*. The soloist, in powerful broad phrases, begins "Sea sunsets, give us keepsakes/Prairie gloamings, pay us for prayers ..." [Example 59]. The song's middle section recalls the changing seasons which to the composer symbolize the unfolding phases of life and which are expressed in a reflective vocal line. Finally the music builds one last time, singer and orchestra joining in an exultant finale, "Give us/Oh, give us great memories!"

In 1976, Warren embarked upon a work celebrating America's Bicentennial, this time for chorus, orchestra and narrator and again using a Sandburg text, *Good Morning, America!* Once more, as with her *Symphony*, the composer abandons strict traditionalism to paint musical pictures in a less conventional way.

Good Morning, America! is Warren's only work that calls for a narrator as soloist, along with the chorus. Throughout, one or the other develop the text, which describes the building of America's great cities by its workers. Sometimes the chorus is treated instrumentally without words, lending added musical color under the narration.

To contrast with the lyrical cadences of Sandburg's poetic style, Warren etches bold, angular harmonies, particularly in the orchestration. The work opens with an impressionistic, mysterious mood established in the orchestra over a long, *sostenuto* E-flat in the low strings that predominates throughout the introductory section. There are occasional short, sharp phrases penetrating the descriptive tranquillity of night. As the chorus enters at the 22nd measure, the pervading undercurrent of the restless city, even in the depths of night, is expressed with a marching rhythm over a rumbling bass [Example 60].

In the middle of the work is a section for orchestra alone, mainly strings and muted brass, which sets the mood for the narrator's introspective telling of the beginnings of America [Example 61]. Then the chorus, first as background to the narrator, further expresses this reminiscent mood, alternating with the narrator in developing, by music and words, the gradual growth and vigor of the nation [Example 62].

Suddenly the chorus bursts in at the latter section, "We are here! We belong! Look at us! Good morning, America!" [Example 63]. Passages follow closely between narrator and chorus, ever building with excitement; later the chorus even calls "Good morning!" to each other and to the audience. Then they break into song again, joyfully proclaiming an extended phrase as they sing, with full orchestra *fortissimo*, a final "Good morning, America!" Over this the narrator shouts the same words, bringing the work to a dynamic finale.

Warren's most recent works mark a period of transition. Inspired earlier by the influence of Nadia Boulanger, yet still shaped by text or visual impression, these compositions more closely reveal the composer's confrontation with the hard-edged world of here and now. Joined with her characteristic craftsmanship, emotional intensity, use of harmonic and rhythmic contrasts, and highly effective climaxes, this further development points the way to an intriguing new dynamic.

Example 1: *Snow Towards Evening,* measures 10-11

Example 2: *The Nights Remember,* measures 15-18

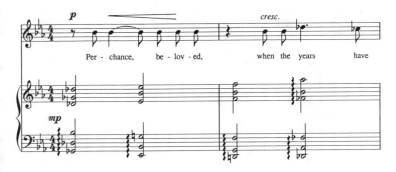

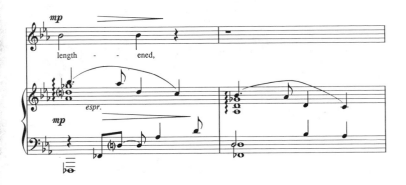

Example 3: *If You Have Forgotten*, measures 3-6

Example 4: *Piano*, measures 5-8

Example 5: *Lonely Roads*, measures 3-6

Example 6: *White Horses of the Sea*, measures 14-18

Example 7: *We Two*, measures 3-6

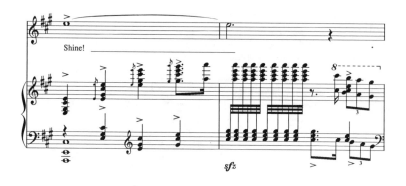

Example 8: *Heather*, measures 2-5

Example 9: *Now Welcome, Summer!*, measures 1-4

Example 10: *On the Echoing Green,* measures 3-7

Example 11: *Praises and Prayers: Christmas Introit,*
           measures 1-2

Example 12: *Praises and Prayers*: *Easter Introit*, measures 8-10

Example 13: *Little Choral Suite: Rain Slippers,* measures
2-5

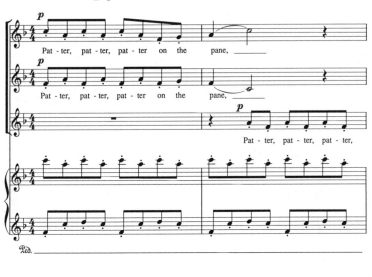

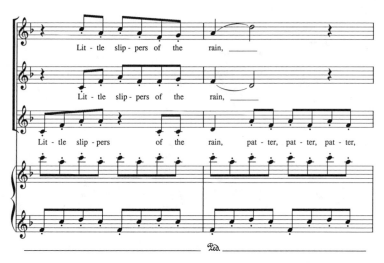

Example 14: *Little Choral Suite: Sleep Walks Over the Hill*, measures 3-6

Example 15: *Little Choral Suite: A Little Song of Life*,
            measures 27-30

Example 16: *White Iris*, measures 1-6

Example 17: *My Heart Is Ready,* measures 3-6

Example 18: *The Night Will Never Stay,* measures 38-42

Example 19: *The Crystal Lake,* measures 5-7

Example 20: *The Crystal Lake,* measures 85-87

Example 21: *Along the Western Shore:* 1st Movement,
             measures 13-14

Example 22: *Along the Western Shore:* 2nd Movement,
             measures 3-6

Example 23: *Along the Western Shore:* 3rd Movement,
             measures 6-9

Example 24: *The Harp Weaver*, measures 208-209

Example 25: *The Harp Weaver*, measures 324-326

Example 26: *The Legend of King Arthur*: King Arthur
         Theme, page 5, 2nd measure before (2)

Example 27: *The Legend of King Arthur*: Excalibur Theme,
         last measure, page 11-first measure, page 12

Example 28: *The Legend of King Arthur*: Lake Waters
         Theme, page 26 at (14)

Example 29: *The Legend of King Arthur*: Barge Theme,
          page 63 at (4)

Example 30: *The Legend of King Arthur*: *Intermezzo*, 1st
          theme, measures 5-8

Example 31: *The Legend of King Arthur*: *Intermezzo*, 2nd
          theme at (1) for 5 measures

Example 32: *The Legend of King Arthur: King Arthur's
          Farewell*, page 81 at 7th measure after (12)

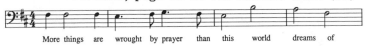

More things are wrought by prayer than this world dreams of

Example 33: *Sonnets for Soprano and String Quartet:*
Sonnet 7, measures 43-44

Example 34: *Sonnets for Soprano and String Quartet:*
Sonnet 11, measures 57-59

Example 35: *Transcontinental,* measures 68-71

Example 36: *Suite for Orchestra*: 1st Movement, measures
10-11

Example 37: *Suite for Orchestra*: 1st Movement, measures
34-37

Example 38: *Suite for Orchestra*: 2nd Movement, measures
42-45

Example 39: *Suite for Orchestra*: 3rd Movement, measures
9-12

Example 40: *Suite for Orchestra*: 3rd Movement, measures
72-75

Example 41: *Suite for Orchestra*: 4th Movement, measures
4-5

Example 42: *Suite for Orchestra*: 4th Movement, measures
90-91

Example 43: *Abram in Egypt,* measures 60-63

Example 44: *Abram in Egypt,* measures 148-152

Example 45: *Abram in Egypt,* measures 380-386

Example 46: *Requiem: Kyrie,* measures 79-80

Example 47: *Requiem: Graduale*, measures 1-4

Example 48: *Requiem: Dies Irae*, measures 20-21

Example 49: *Requiem: Dies Irae*, measures 145-148

Example 50: *Requiem: Offertorium*, measures 1-4

Example 51: *Requiem: Sanctus,* measures 34-35

Example 52: *Requiem: Lux Aeterna,* measures 78-81

Example 53: *Symphony in One Movement*, Violins I,
            measures 8-11

Example 54: *Symphony in One Movement*, measures 260-
            263

Example 55: *Symphony in One Movement*, Violins I,
            measures 306-308

Example 56: *Singing Earth: The Wind Sings Welcome*,
            measures 76-81

Have you seen such flick-ing heels be - fore, _____

Sil - ver Jig heels on the pur - ple sky   rim?

Example 57: *Singing Earth: Summer Stars,* measures 139-
144

Bend ____ low,   bend ____ low a - gain,

Night ____ of stars,   oh,   night _____ of sum - mer stars! _____

Example 58: *Singing Earth: Tawny Days*, measures 202-210

Tawn - y days___   and   your face   a - gain! _____

your ___ face _____ a - - gain. ___

Example 59: *Singing Earth: Great Memories*, measures 236-
240

Sea   sun - sets,   give us keep - sakes,

Prair - ie gloam - ings,   pay us   for pray'rs,

Example 60: *Good Morning, America!*, measures 28-29

Example 61: *Good Morning, America!*, measures 178-179

Example 62: *Good Morning, America!*, measures 215-218

Look   back,   look   back,   and that was long   a - go

Example 63: *Good Morning, America!*, measures 283-284

Good   morn - ing A - mer - i - ca!

CATALOG OF THE WORKS OF ELINOR REMICK WARREN

Key to Annotations for Catalog Entries (Listed alphabetically within classifications by number and title; each choral work or song designated as *sacred* or *secular*.)

R	Recording available (commercial or in library archive)
Text	Author of text
Pub	Publisher
Comm	Commission
Grant	Funding source
Date	Date of publication or completion of manuscript
Copy	Copyright information
Prem	Premiere performance
Key	Voice range of song
Parts	Choral parts
Acc	Accompaniment
Inst	Instrumentation
Solo	Solo part(s)
Narr	Narrator
Loc	Location of copies (including works active with publishers or libraries holding copy or copies of work)
Time	Timing
Ded	Dedication
Prize	Prize won in competition

Terms and Sigla

SATB	Choral music for soprano, alto, tenor and bass voices
SSAA, SSA,SA	Choral music for women's voices
TTBB	Choral music for men's voices

AMC   American Music Center, New York, New York

AWC   American Women Composers, Inc., Washington, DC

National Union Catalogue Designations

LAPL   Los Angeles Public Library
NN   New York Public Library
PP   Free Library of Philadelphia
PP(FC)   Free Library of Philadelphia, Edwin A. Fleisher Collection of Orchestral Music
CLSU   University of Southern California
DLC   Library of Congress
CLU   University of California at Los Angeles (UCLA)
PPCI   Curtis Institute of Music
IU   University of Illinois, Urbana
OrP   Library Association of Portland (Oregon)
RPB   Brown University, Providence
IEN   Northwestern University, Evanston
FTaSU   Florida State University, Tallahassee
MB   Boston Public Library
MiU   University of Michigan, Ann Arbor

Works for Orchestra

1. *Along the Western Shore* - R

   Pub   Carl Fischer, New York
   Date   1954 (originally composed as three pieces for piano, 1946-47)
   Copy   1978
   Prem   October 31, 1954, Los Angeles; Los Angeles Philharmonic, John Barnett, conductor
   Inst   2(Picc.)-2(Eng. Hn.)-2(Bass Cl.)-2(Con. Bsn.); 4-2-3-1; Timp., 2 Perc., Hp., Cel.; Str.
   Loc   Carl Fischer, New York (Rental Library); NN, PP(FC), AWC
   Time   11 minutes

2. *The Crystal Lake* - R

Pub	Carl Fischer, New York
Date	1946
Copy	1978
Prem	March 21, 1946, Los Angeles; Los Angeles Philharmonic, Alfred Wallenstein, conductor
Inst	2(Picc.)-2(Eng. Hn.)-2-2; 4-2-3-0; Timp., Hp., 2 Perc., Cel.; Str.
Loc	Carl Fischer, New York (Rental Library); NN, PP(FC), AWC
Time	9.5 minutes

3. *The Fountain* - R

Date	1939 (originally composed for piano, 1934)
Copy	1985
Prem	June, 1940, Pasadena, CA; Pasadena Civic Orchestra, Richard Lert, conductor
Inst	2-2-2-2; 3-2-3-0; Timp., Cel., 2 Perc., Hp.; Str.
Loc	NN, PP(FC), AWC
Time	4 minutes

4. *Intermezzo* (from *The Legend of King Arthur*) - R

Pub	Carl Fischer, New York (originally H.W. Gray)
Date	1940
Copy	1939; 1974 (revised edition of full work); 1978
Prem	March 18, 1939, Pasadena, CA; Pasadena Civic Orchestra, Richard Lert, conductor
Inst	3-2-Eng. Hn.-2-Bass Cl.-2; 4-3-3-1; Timp., Hp., Perc.; Str.
Loc	Carl Fischer, New York (Rental Library); NN, PP(FC), AWC
Time	4.5 minutes

5. *Scherzo* - R

Date	1950 (originally composed for piano as *Frolic of the Elves*, 1937)
Copy	1985

Prem	Winter, 1937, Los Angeles; KHJ Radio Orchestra, Mutual Broadcasting System
Inst	2-2-2-2; 3-2-3-0; Cel., Timp., Hp., 2 Perc.; Str.
Loc	NN, PP(FC), AWC
Time	2 minutes

6. *Suite for Orchestra - R*

   a. Allegro Moderato - *Black Cloud Horses*
   b. Andante Molto Tranquillo - *Cloud Peaks*
   c. Scherzino: Allegretto - *Ballet of the Midsummer Sky*
   d. Moderato - *Pageant Across the Sky*

Pub	Carl Fischer, New York
Date	1954; revised 1960
Copy	1978
Prem	March 3, 1955, Los Angeles; Los Angeles Philharmonic, Alfred Wallenstein, conductor
Inst	2(Picc.)-2-2-2; 4-2-3-1; Timp., Hp., 2 Perc.; Str.
Loc	Carl Fischer, New York (Rental Library); DLC (CRI recording only); NN, PP(FC), AWC
Time	17 minutes

7. *Symphony in One Movement - R*

Pub	Carl Fischer, New York
Comm	Stanford University
Date	1970
Copy	1978
Prem	December 6, 1970, Palo Alto, CA; Stanford University Orchestra, Sanford Salgo, conductor
Inst	2(Picc.)-2(Eng. Hn.)-2-2; 4-2-3-1; Timp., Hp., Cel., 2 Perc.; Str.
Loc	Carl Fischer, New York (Rental Library); NN, PP(FC), AWC
Time	16 minutes

Works for Orchestra and Soloist

8. *Abram in Egypt*

Text	Dead Sea Scrolls and Book of Genesis
Pub	Carl Fischer, New York
Comm	Louis Sudler
Date	1959
Copy	1962; 1978
Prem	April 19, 1959, Chicago; Northwestern University Orchestra, Thor Johnson, conductor; Louis Sudler, baritone soloist
Inst	2(Picc.)-2-2-2(Con. Bsn.); 4-2-3-1; Timp., Hp., 2 Perc.; Str.
Solo	Baritone
Loc	Carl Fischer, New York (Rental Library); NN, PP(FC)
Time	23 minutes

9. *Christmas Candle*

Text	Kate Louise Brown
Pub	Manuscript
Date	Circa 1960
Inst	Vln. 1, Vln. 2, Cello, Hp. or Pno.; Cel.; Organ; Flute
Solo	Soprano or Tenor
Loc	Composer

10. *Down in the Glen*

Text	Katharine Adams
Pub	Manuscript
Date	Circa 1940's
Inst	2-2-2-2; 4 Hns.; Hp.; Bells; Str.
Solo	Soprano
Loc	Composer

11. *Dreams*

Text	Beatrice Fenner
Pub	Manuscript
Date	Circa 1940's
Inst	2-2-2-2; 2 Hns.; Hp.; Vibraph.; Str.
Solo	Soprano

   Loc Composer

12. *The Heart of a Rose*

   Text Alfred Noyes
   Pub Manuscript
   Date Circa 1940's
   Inst 2-2-2-2; 4-2-3-0; Hp.; Str.
   Solo Soprano
   Loc Composer

13. *King Arthur's Farewell* (aria from *The Legend of King Arthur*) - R

   Text Alfred Tennyson
   Pub Carl Fischer, New York (originally H.W. Gray)
   Key High, Low
   Date 1941
   Copy 1941; renewed 1969
   Prem November 26, 1941, Washington, DC; National Symphony Orchestra, Hans Kindler, conductor; Richard Crooks, soloist
   Inst 3(Picc.)-2-Eng. Hn.-2-Bass Cl.-2; 4-3-3-1; Timp., 2 Perc., Hp.; Str.
   Solo Tenor or Baritone
   Loc Carl Fischer, New York (Rental Library); NN, PP(FC)
   Time 5 minutes

14. *Lady Lo-Fu* (originally *My Lady Lo-Fu*)

   Text Mona Modini Wood
   Pub Manuscript
   Date Circa 1940's
   Inst 2-2-2-2; 2 Hns.; Hp.; Sm. Bells; Cymb.; Str.
   Solo Soprano
   Loc Composer

15. *The Little Betrothed*

   Text Isabel Hume
   Pub Manuscript
   Date Circa 1940's

Inst   1-1-2-1; 2 Hns.; Bells & Cel. (optional);
         Hp.; Str.
Solo   Soprano
Loc   Composer

16. *Silent Noon*

Text   Dante Gabriel Rossetti
Pub   Manuscript
Date   Circa 1940's
Inst   2-2-2-2; 2 Hns.; Cel.; Hp.; Str.
Solo   Soprano or Tenor
Loc   Composer

17. *Singing Earth - R*

Text   Carl Sandburg
Pub   Carl Fischer, New York
Date   1950; revised 1978
Copy   1950; renewed 1978 (revised edition)
Prem   May 30, 1952; Ojai Festival, Ojai, CA; Ojai
         Festival Orchestra, Thor Johnson, conductor;
         Rose Bampton, soloist
Inst   2(Picc.)-2(Eng. Hn.)-2-2; 4-2-3-0; Timp.,
         Hp., Cel., 2 Perc.; Str.
Loc   Carl Fischer, New York (Rental Library);
         NN, PP(FC), AWC
Time   15 minutes

18. *Sonnets for Soprano and String Orchestra - R*

Text   Edna St. Vincent Millay (*Fatal Interview -
         Sonnets 7, 11, 35, 52*)
Pub   Carl Fischer, New York
Date   1954
Copy   1974
Prem   April 28, 1963, Royce Hall, UCLA; NAACC
         Orchestra, H. Arthur Brown, conductor;
         Christina Carroll, soloist
Inst   Vlns. 1, Vlns. 2, Vlas., Celli, Dle. Bass
Loc   Carl Fischer, New York (Rental Library);
         NN, PP(FC), AWC, DLC
Time   15 minutes

19. *Time, You Old Gypsy-Man*

    Text   Ralph Hodgson
    Pub   Manuscript
    Date   Circa 1940's
    Inst   2-2-2-2; 4-2-3-0; 1 Perc. (Tri., Bells, Tamb.), Timp., Harp; Str.
    Solo   Soprano or Tenor
    Loc   Composer

Works for Orchestra and Chorus, or Orchestra, Chorus and Soloist(s)

20. *Abram in Egypt - R*

    Text   Dead Sea Scrolls and Book of Genesis
    Pub   Carl Fischer, New York (originally H.W. Gray)
    Comm   Louis Sudler
    Date   1959
    Copy   1962; 1978
    Prem   June 7, 1961, Los Angeles; Los Angeles International Music Festival, Royce Hall, UCLA; Roger Wagner Chorale and Festival Orchestra, Roger Wagner, conductor; Donald Gramm, soloist
    Parts   SATB
    Inst   2(Picc.)-2-2-2(Con. Bsn.); 4-2-3-1; Timp., Hp., 2 Perc.; Str.
    Solo   Baritone
    Loc   Carl Fischer, New York (Rental Library); DLC (CRI recording only), NN, PP(FC), AMC, AWC
    Time   23 minutes
    Prize   Gedok International Competition for Women Composers, Mannheim, Germany; Second Prize, Vocal Category

21. *Good Morning, America! - R*

    Text   Carl Sandburg
    Pub   Carl Fischer, New York
    Comm   Occidental College, Los Angeles (for 1976 Bicentennial)

Grant	National Endowment for the Arts Fellowship, 1976
Date	1976
Copy	1976
Prem	November 21, 1976, California State University, Fullerton, CA; University Orchestra and Chorale, Dr. Howard Swan, conductor; Roger Ardrey, narrator
Parts	SATB
Inst	A Score: 2(Picc.)-2(Eng. Hn.)-2-2; 2-2-2-0; Timp., 2 Perc., Pno.(Cel.); Str. B Score: Augmented Brass: 4-2-3-1
Narr	Narrator
Loc	Carl Fischer, New York (Rental Library); NN, PP(FC), LAPL, AMC, AWC, CLU, DLC
Time	16 minutes

22. *The Harp Weaver*

Text	Edna St. Vincent Millay
Pub	Carl Fischer, New York (originally H.W. Gray)
Date	1932
Copy	1932; renewed 1960; 1978
Prem	c.1935, Los Angeles; Cecilian Singers, Symphonia Praeceptorum, John Smallman, conductor; Alan Watson, soloist
Parts	SSA
Inst	2(Picc.)-2(Eng. Hn.)-2-2; 4-2-3-1; Timp., 2 Perc., Hp.; Str.
Solo	Baritone
Loc	Carl Fischer, New York (Rental Library); NN, PP(FC), LAPL, AWC, CLU, RPB, IEN
Time	15 minutes

23. *The Legend of King Arthur* (originally *The Passing of King Arthur*) - R

Text	Alfred Tennyson (*Idylls of the King*: *The Passing of Arthur*)
Pub	Carl Fischer, New York (originally H.W. Gray)
Date	1939
Copy	1939; 1974 (revised edition); 1978

Prem	March 21, 1940, Los Angeles; Los Angeles Philharmonic Orchestra, Los Angeles Oratorio Society, Albert Coates, conductor; Paul Keast, baritone, and David Laughlin, tenor
Parts	SATB
Inst	3(Picc.)-2-Eng. Hn.-2-Bass Cl.-2; 4-3-3-1; Timp., 3 Perc., Hp.; Str.
Solo	Baritone and Tenor
Loc	Carl Fischer, New York (Rental Library); NN, PP(FC), LAPL, AWC, CLU, DLC, MB, MiU
Time	60 minutes
Ded	"Dedicated to my Mother and Father"

24. *Now Welcome, Summer!*

Text	Geoffrey Chaucer
Pub	Lawson-Gould, New York
Date	1984
Copy	1984
Parts	SATB
Inst	1-1-2-1; 2-1-0-0; Str.
Loc	Lawson-Gould, New York (Rental Library); NN, PP, AWC
Time	3 minutes

25. *On the Echoing Green*

Text	William Blake
Pub	Lawson-Gould, New York
Date	1985
Copy	1987
Parts	SATB
Inst	1-1-2-1; 2-1-0-0; Str.
Loc	Lawson-Gould, New York (Rental Library)
Time	4 minutes

26. *Our Beloved Land*

Text	Samuel Bonner
Pub	Theodore Presser, Bryn Mawr, PA
Date	1958 (Carillon Theme); 1963 (Complete Work)
Copy	1963

Prem	Carillon Theme: August 30, 1958, Hollywood Bowl; Chimes and Roger Wagner Chorale, Los Angeles Philharmonic Orchestra, John Green, conductor
Prem	Complete Work: Hollywood Bowl, August 10, 1963; Jack Halloran Singers, Hollywood Bowl Orchestra, John Scott Trotter, conductor
Parts	SATB
Inst	2-2-2-2; 4-2-3-1; Timp., Cym.; Str.
Loc	Theodore Presser, Bryn Mawr, PA (Rental Library); NN, PP(FC), AWC
Time	2.5 minutes

27. *Requiem - R*

    a. *Introit and Kyrie*
    b. *Graduale*
    c. *Dies Irae*
    d. *Offertorium*
    e. *Hostias*
    f. *Sanctus (Hosanna)*
    g. *Benedictus (Hosanna)*
    h. *Agnus Dei*
    i. *Lux Aeterna*

Text	Latin (English text from the Liturgy, trans. by composer)
Pub	Carl Fischer, New York (originally published by Lawson-Gould)
Comm	Roger Wagner
Date	1965
Copy	1965
Prem	April 3, 1966, Dorothy Chandler Pavilion, Los Angeles Music Center; Los Angeles Master Chorale and Sinfonia Orchestra, Roger Wagner, conductor; soloists Carol Neblett, soprano, and Paul Hinshaw, baritone
Parts	SATB
Inst	2(Picc.)-2(Eng. Hn.)-2-2; 4-2-3-1; Timp., 2 Perc., Cel., Hp.; Str.
Solo	Soprano and Baritone

> *Loc*   Carl Fischer, New York (Rental Library);
>   NN, PP(FC), AWC, CLU, DLC
> *Time*   53 minutes
> *Ded*   "To Roger Wagner"

28. *Sanctus* (from *Requiem*) (includes *Benedictus* &
    Hosanna)

> *Text*   Latin (English text from the Liturgy, trans.
>   by composer)
> *Pub*   Lawson-Gould, New York
> *Date*   1966
> *Copy*   1965
> *Prem*   June 10, 1979, Schoenberg Hall, UCLA;
>   Roger Wagner Chorale and Sinfonia Chamber
>   Ensemble, Roger Wagner, conductor
> *Parts* SATB
> *Inst*   Strings, timp., piano or organ
> *Solo*   Baritone
> *Loc*   Lawson-Gould, New York; NN, PP(FC), AWC
> *Time*   6.5 minutes

29. *The Sleeping Beauty*

> a. *The Sleeping Palace*
> b. *The Sleeping Princess*
> c. *The Prince's Arrival*
> d. *The Awakening*
> e. *The King and Lords*
> f. *The Departure*

> *Text*   Alfred Tennyson
> *Pub*   H.W. Gray, New York
> *Date*   1951
> *Copy*   1951; renewed 1979
> *Parts* SATB
> *Inst*   2(Picc.)-1-2-1; 2-2-3-0; Timp., Pno., Perc.;
>   Str.
> *Solo*   Soprano, Baritone and Bass-Baritone
> *Loc*   NN, PP(FC), LAPL, DLC
> *Time*   18 minutes

30. *To My Native Land*

> *Text*   Henry Wadsworth Longfellow

Pub	E.C. Schirmer, Boston
Date	1944 (orchestration)
Copy	1942; renewed 1969
Parts	SSAA TTBB
Inst	2-2-2-2; 4-2-3-0; Timp., Cym., Hp.; Str.
Loc	E.C. Schirmer, Boston
Time	3.5 minutes

31. *Transcontinental - R*

Text	A.M. Sullivan
Pub	Theodore Presser, Bryn Mawr, PA
Date	1958
Copy	1958; renewed 1986
Prem	May 26, 1958, Occidental College, Los Angeles; Occidental College Chorus & Orchestra, Dr. Howard Swan, conductor
Parts	SATB
Inst	2(Picc.)-1-2-1; 2-2-2-0; Timp., 2 Perc., Pno.; Str.
Solo	Baritone
Loc	Theodore Presser, Bryn Mawr, PA (Rental Library); NN, PP, AWC
Time	11.5 minutes
Ded	"To Howard Swan and the Occidental College Glee Clubs"

Works for Chamber Group

32. *Quintet for Woodwinds and Horn*

Pub	Manuscript
Date	Circa 1935-36
Prem	January 23, 1940, San Francisco; San Francisco Woodwind Quintette
Inst	Fl., Ob., Cl., Bssn., Hn.
Loc	Composer

33. *Sonnets for Soprano and String Quartet*

Text	Edna St. Vincent Millay (from *Fatal Interview* - Sonnets 7, 11, 35, 52)
Pub	Carl Fischer, New York
Date	1954

Copy   1974
Prem   September 26, 1954, Los Angeles County
          Museum of Art; Musart String Quartet,
          Patricia Beems, soloist
Inst   Vln. 1, Vln. 2, Vla., Cello
Loc   Carl Fischer, New York (Rental Library);
          NN, PP, AWC, CLU, DLC
Time   15 minutes

Works for Instrumental Solo

34. *Dark Hills* (piano)

    Pub   Carl Fischer, New York
    Date   1946
    Copy   1946; renewed 1974
    Loc   Carl Fischer, NY; NN, PP, CLU

35. *Concert Transcriptions of Three Stephen Foster Melodies* (piano)

    a. *Jeannie with the Light Brown Hair*
    b. *Beautiful Dreamer*
    c. *De Camptown Races*

    Pub   Oliver Ditson, Philadelphia
    Date   1940
    Copy   1940; renewed 1968
    Loc   NN, PP, CLU

36. *The Fountain* (piano)

    Pub   G. Schirmer, New York
    Date   1934
    Copy   1934; renewed 1961
    Loc   NN, PP, LAPL, AWC, CLU

37. *Frolic of the Elves* (piano)

    Pub   Harold Flammer, New York
    Date   1924
    Copy   1924; renewed 1952
    Loc   DLC, NN, PP, LAPL
    Ded   "To Ernesto Berumen"

38. *If Thou Art Near* (transcribed from a Bach air, for piano)

   Pub   Harold Flammer, New York
   Date   1939
   Copy   1939; renewed 1967
   Loc   NN, PP

39. *Poem* (piano)

   Pub   Carl Fischer, New York
   Date   1946
   Copy   1946; renewed 1974
   Loc   Carl Fischer, NY; NN, PP, CLU

40. *Poem* (viola and piano)

   Pub   Carl Fischer, New York
   Date   1948
   Copy   1948; renewed 1976
   Prem   1944, on national tour; William Primrose, viola
   Loc   Carl Fischer, NY; NN, PP, CLU, DLC
   Ded   "To William Primrose"

41. *Processional March* (organ) - R

   Pub   G. Schirmer, New York
   Date   1969
   Copy   1969
   Loc   G. Schirmer, New York; NN, PP, AWC, CLSU

42. *Sea Rhapsody* (piano)

   Pub   Carl Fischer, New York
   Date   1946
   Copy   1946; renewed 1974
   Loc   Carl Fischer, NY; NN, PP, CLU

Works for Chorus SATB, Accompanied

43. *Arise, My Heart and Sing!* (sacred)

   Text   Richard Le Gallienne

Pub	H.W. Gray, New York
Acc	Organ
Date	1922
Copy	1922; renewed 1950
Loc	NN, PP
Ded	"To the Rev. Hugh K. Walker, D.D."

44. *Awake! Put on Strength!* (sacred)

Text	Isaiah 51:9-11
Pub	Concordia, St. Louis, MO
Acc	Organ
Date	1967
Copy	1967
Loc	NN, PP, AWC

45. *Because of Thy Great Bounty* (sacred)

Text	Grace Noll Crowell
Pub	H.W. Gray, New York
Acc	Organ or Piano
Date	1937
Copy	1937; renewed 1965
Loc	NN, PP

46. *Christmas Candle* (sacred/secular) - *R*

Text	Kate Louise Brown
Pub	G. Schirmer, New York
Acc	Organ or Piano
Date	1940
Copy	1940; renewed 1968
Solo	Soprano
Loc	NN, PP
Ded	"To Jimmy, Wayne, Jr., and Elayne"

47. *Christmas Morn* (sacred)

Text	1st & 2nd verses by Grace Widney Mabee; 3rd verse by Agnes Moulton
Pub	Harold Flammer, New York
Acc	Organ or Piano (optional violin obbligato)
Date	1922
Copy	1922; renewed 1950
Loc	NN, PP

Note   Also published for unison voices

48. *Christ Went Up Into the Hills* (sacred)

Text	Katharine Adams
Pub	H.W. Gray, New York
Acc	Organ or Piano
Date	1922
Copy	1922; renewed 1950
Solo	Soprano or Tenor
Loc	NN, PP
Ded	"To Clarence Dickinson"

49. *Come to the Stable* (with children's chorus) (sacred)

Text	Jane Miller Manning
Pub	H.W. Gray, New York
Acc	Organ
Date	1958
Copy	1958; renewed 1986
Loc	AWCL

50. *From Glory Unto Glory* (sacred)

Text	F.R. Haragal (Episcopal Hymnal)
Pub	Harold Flammer, New York
Acc	Organ
Date	1922
Copy	1922; renewed 1950
Loc	NN, PP

51. *God is My Song!* (sacred)

Text	Isaiah, 12th Chapter
Pub	Boosey-Hawkes, New York
Acc	Organ
Date	1963
Copy	1963
Loc	Boosey-Hawkes, New York; NN, PP, AWC
Ded	"To William C. Hartshorn, and the choir of the First Methodist Church of Pasadena, California"

52. *Hark! What Mean Those Holy Voices?* (sacred)

  Text Rev. John Cawood
  Pub Enoch & Sons, New York
  Acc Organ
  Date 1925
  Copy 1925; renewed 1952
  Loc NN, PP

53. *Hosanna to the Living Lord!* (sacred)

  Text Reginald Heber (from the Hymnal)
  Pub H.W. Gray, New York
  Acc Organ
  Date 1929
  Copy 1929; renewed 1957
  Loc NN, PP

54. *Hymn of the City* (secular)

  Text William Cullen Bryant
  Pub Carl Fischer, New York
  Acc Organ
  Date 1970
  Copy 1970
  Loc Composer

55. *Jesus, from Thy Throne on High* (sacred)

  Text Thomas B. Pollock (from the Hymnal)
  Pub H.W. Gray, New York
  Acc Organ
  Date 1924
  Copy 1924; renewed 1952
  Loc NN, PP, LAPL

56. *A Joyful Song of Praise* (sacred)

  Text Isaiah 25
  Pub Harold Flammer, New York
  Acc Organ
  Date 1966
  Copy 1966
  Loc Composer

57. *Let the Heavens Praise Thy Wonders* (sacred)

    Text   Adapted from Psalm 89
    Pub   H.W. Gray, New York
    Acc   Organ
    Date 1974
    Copy 1974
    Loc   NN, PP, AWC

58. *My Heart Is Ready* (sacred)

    Text   Psalm 108
    Pub   Lawson-Gould, New York
    Acc   Organ
    Date 1967
    Copy 1969
    Loc   Lawson-Gould, New York; NN, PP, AWC

59. *Night Rider* (secular)

    Text   Robert Louis Stevenson
    Pub   Lawson-Gould, New York
    Acc   Piano
    Date 1975
    Copy 1975
    Loc   Lawson-Gould, New York; NN, PP, AWC

60. *Now Thank We All Our God* (sacred)

    Text   Martin Rinkart (tr. Catherine Winkworth)
    Pub   Fred Bock, Tarzana, CA
    Acc   Organ
    Date 1981
    Copy 1981
    Loc   NN, PP, AWC

61. *Now Welcome, Summer!* (secular)

    Text   Geoffrey Chaucer
    Pub   Lawson-Gould, New York
    Acc   Piano
    Date 1984
    Copy 1984
    Loc   Lawson-Gould, New York; NN, PP, AWC

62. *On the Echoing Green* (secular)

  Text William Blake
  Pub Lawson-Gould, New York
  Acc Piano
  Date 1985
  Copy 1987
  Loc Lawson-Gould, New York

63. *Our Beloved Land* (secular)

  Text Samuel Bonner
  Pub Theodore Presser, Bryn Mawr, PA
  Acc Piano
  Date 1963
  Copy 1963
  Loc Theodore Presser, Bryn Mawr, PA (Rental
     Library); NN, PP

64. *Praises and Prayers* (Seven Introits, Prayer
Responses and Benedictions) (sacred)

 a. Introits:
  All Glory to Our Lord! - Text: The Book of
   Common Prayer;
  A Christmas Introit (Christians, Awake!) - Text:
   John Byrom (18th Century);
  An Easter Introit - Text: The Book of Common
   Prayer
 b. Prayer Responses and Benedictions:
  Of Thy Goodness, Give Us - Text: Ancient
   Collect;
  Let Thy Servant Depart in Peace - Text: Luke
   2:29;
  Lord, Dismiss Us with Thy Blessing - Text: John
   Fawcett (1773);
  Benediction (The Peace of God) - Text: The
   Book of Common Prayer

  Pub Neil Kjos, San Diego, CA
  Acc Organs; optional brass accompaniment
     published separately
  Date 1981
  Copy 1982
  Loc Neil Kjos, San Diego, CA; NN, PP

65. *Sanctus* (from *Requiem*) (sacred)

    Text   Latin (English text from the Liturgy, trans.
             by composer)
    Pub   Lawson-Gould, New York
    Acc   Organ or Piano
    Date   1966
    Copy 1965
    Loc   Lawson-Gould, New York; NN, PP, AWC

66. *Soldiers of Christ, Arise!* (sacred)

    Text   Charles Wesley
    Pub   H.W. Gray, New York
    Acc   Organ
    Date   1923
    Copy 1923; renewed 1951
    Loc   NN, PP
    Ded   "To My Father"

67. *Time, You Old Gypsy-Man* (secular)

    Text   Ralph Hodgson
    Pub   Neil Kjos, San Diego, CA
    Acc   Piano
    Date   1981
    Copy 1981
    Loc   Neil Kjos, San Diego, CA; NN, PP, AWC

68. *To the Farmer* (secular)

    Text   Inscription on the jug *Farmer's Arms*
    Pub   Carl Fischer, New York
    Acc   Piano
    Date   1955
    Copy 1955; renewed 1983
    Loc   Carl Fischer, New York; NN, PP, LAPL

Works for Chorus SATB, a Cappella

69. *At Midnight* (secular)

    Text   James Russell Lowell
    Pub   H.W. Gray, New York
    Date   1936

> *Copy*   1936; renewed 1964
> *Loc*   NN, PP
> *Ded*   "To Mr. Harry C. Banks, Jr. and the Choral
> Art Society of Philadelphia"

70. *Autumn Sunset in the Canyon* (from *Four Songs of the Seasons*) (secular)

> *Text*   Mona Modini Wood
> *Pub*   H.W. Gray, New York
> *Date*   1929
> *Copy*   1929; renewed 1957
> *Loc*   NN, PP, LAPL
> *Ded*   "To the Smallman A Cappella Choir"

71. *The Christ Child Smiled* (sacred)

> *Text*   Katharine Adams
> *Pub*   H.W. Gray, New York
> *Date*   1923
> *Copy*   1923; renewed 1951
> *Loc*   NN, PP, LAPL

72. *Christmas Candle* (sacred/secular)

> *Text*   Kate Louise Brown
> *Pub*   G. Schirmer, New York
> *Date*   1940
> *Copy*   1940; renewed 1968
> *Solo*   Soprano
> *Loc*   NN, PP

73. *Everywhere, Everywhere, Christmas Tonight!* (sacred)

> *Text*   Phillips Brooks
> *Pub*   G. Schirmer, New York
> *Date*   1937
> *Copy*   1937; renewed 1965
> *Loc*   Composer

74. *The Gate of the Year* (sacred/secular)

> *Text*   M. Louise Haskins
> *Pub*   Harold Flammer, New York
> *Date*   1967

Copy   1967
Loc   Composer

75. *God Be in My Heart* (sacred)

Text   Anonymous, 16th century
Pub   Oliver Ditson, Philadelphia
Date   1950
Copy   1950; renewed 1978
Loc   LAPL

76. *In the Day of Battle* (sacred)

Text   Bliss Carman
Pub   Galaxy Music, New York
Date   1945
Copy   1945; renewed 1972
Loc   NN, PP

77. *More Things Are Wrought By Prayer* (from *The Legend of King Arthur*) (sacred)

Text   Alfred Tennyson
Pub   Carl Fischer, New York
Date   1940
Copy   1939; renewed 1967
Loc   Carl Fischer, New York; NN, PP, AWC

78. *O Hand Unseen* (sacred)

Text   Edward Davison
Pub   H.W. Gray, New York
Date   1933
Copy   1933; renewed 1961
Loc   NN, PP
Ded   "To John C. Wilcox and the Denver A Cappella Choir"

79. *Praises and Prayers* (Seven Introits, Prayer Responses and Benedictions) (sacred)

a. Introits:
   All Glory to Our Lord! - Text: The Book of Common Prayer;
   A Christmas Introit (Christians, Awake!) - Text: John Byrom (18th Century);

An Easter Introit - Text: The Book of Common
     Prayer
b. Prayer Responses and Benedictions:
     Of Thy Goodness, Give us - Text: Ancient
          Collect;
     Let Thy Servant Depart in Peace - Text: Luke
          2:29;
     Lord, Dismiss Us with Thy Blessing - Text: John
          Fawcett (1773);
     Benediction (The Peace of God) - Text: The
          Book of Common Prayer

Pub	Neil Kjos, San Diego, CA
Date	1981
Copy	1982
Loc	Neil Kjos, San Diego, CA; NN, PP

80. *Prayer of St. Francis* (sacred)

Text	Text attributed to St. Francis of Assisi
Pub	H.W. Gray, New York
Date	1948
Copy	1948; renewed 1976
Parts	Double chorus or double quartet
Loc	NN, PP

81. *Rolling Rivers, Dreaming Forests* (secular)

Text	Robert Nathan
Pub	Carl Fischer, New York
Date	1953
Copy	1953; renewed 1981
Loc	NN, PP, AWC

82. *Spring Morning in the Hills* (from *Four Songs of
     the Seasons*) (secular)

Text	Mona Modini Wood
Pub	H.W. Gray, New York
Date	1929
Copy	1929; renewed 1957
Loc	NN, PP, LAPL
Ded	"To the Smallman A Cappella Choir"

83. *Summer Noon on the Desert* (from *Four Songs of the Seasons*) (secular)

    Text   Mona Modini Wood
    Pub   H.W. Gray, New York
    Date   1929
    Copy   1929; renewed 1957
    Loc   NN, PP, LAPL
    Ded   "To the Smallman A Cappella Choir"

84. *To My Native Land* (secular)

    Text   Henry W. Longfellow
    Pub   E.C. Schirmer, Boston
    Date   1942
    Copy   1942; renewed 1969
    Loc   E.C. Schirmer, Boston; NN, PP, AWC
    Ded   "To the A Cappella Choir of The University of California, at Los Angeles, and Raymond Moremen, Director"

85. *Winter Night in the Valley* (from *Four Songs of the Seasons*) (secular)

    Text   Mona Modini Wood
    Pub   H.W. Gray, New York
    Date   1929
    Copy   1929; renewed 1957
    Loc   NN, PP, LAPL
    Ded   "To the Smallman A Cappella Choir"

Works for Men's Chorus TTBB, Piano Accompaniment

86. *Autumn Sunset in the Canyon* (from *Four Songs of the Seasons*) (secular)

    Text   Mona Modini Wood
    Pub   H.W. Gray, New York
    Date   1933
    Copy   1933; renewed 1961
    Loc   NN, PP

87. *Christmas Candle* (sacred/secular)

    Text   Kate Louise Brown

Pub   G. Schirmer, New York
Date   1940
Copy   1940; renewed 1968
Loc   NN, PP
Ded   "To Jimmy, Wayne, and Elayne"

88. *The Full Heart* (secular)

Text   Robert Nichols
Pub   H.W. Gray, New York
Date   1932
Copy   1932; renewed 1960
Loc   NN, PP

89. *Merry-Go-Round* (secular)

Text   Archibald MacLeish
Pub   H.W. Gray, New York
Date   1934
Copy   1934; renewed 1962
Loc   Composer

90. *Sleep* (secular)

Text   Grace Fallow Norton
Pub   G. Schirmer, New York
Date   1934
Copy   1934; renewed 1961
Loc   NN, PP, RPB

91. *Sweetgrass Range* (secular)

Text   Edwin Ford Piper
Pub   Carl Fischer, New York
Date   1934
Copy   1934; renewed 1962
Loc   NN, PP

92. *Two Trees* (secular)

Text   Irene Maunder
Pub   Carl Fischer, New York
Date   1930
Copy   1930; renewed 1957
Loc   NN, PP

Ded   "Dedicated to the Orpheus Club of Los
           Angeles"

93. *White Horses of the Sea* (secular)

Text   Hamish Hendry
Pub   G. Schirmer, New York
Date   1932
Copy   1933; renewed 1961
Loc   NN, PP

94. *Windy Nights* (secular)

Text   Robert Louis Stevenson
Pub   Harold Flammer, New York
Date   1964
Copy   1964
Loc   Composer

Works for Men's Chorus TTBB, a Cappella

95. *At the Crossroads* (secular)

Text   Richard Hovey
Pub   H.W. Gray, New York
Date   1934
Copy   1934; renewed 1962
Loc   NN, PP

96. *The Beautiful Town by the Sea* (secular)

Text   Henry Wadsworth Longfellow
Pub   H.W. Gray, New York
Date   1940
Copy   1940; renewed 1968
Loc   NN, PP
Ded   "To the Cantando Club of Santa Ana, and
           Joseph J. Klein, director"

97. *Do You Fear the Wind?* (secular)

Text   Hamlin Garland
Pub   Carl Fischer, New York
Date   1937
Copy   1937; renewed 1964

> *Loc*   NN, PP
> *Ded*   "To Mr. Howard Swan and the Occidental
>   College Men's Glee Club"

Works for Women's Chorus, Piano Accompaniment

98. *Autumn Sunset in the Canyon* (from *Four Songs of the Seasons*) (secular)

> *Text*   Mona Modini Wood
> *Pub*   H.W. Gray, New York
> *Date*   1928
> *Copy*   1928; renewed 1956
> *Parts*   SSA
> *Loc*   NN, PP

99. *By A Fireside* (secular)

> *Text*   Thomas Jones, Jr.
> *Pub*   G. Schirmer, New York
> *Date*   1944
> *Copy*   1944; renewed 1972
> *Parts*   SSA
> *Loc*   NN, PP

100. *Children of the Moon* (secular)

> *Text*   Katharine Adams
> *Pub*   Harold Flammer, New York
> *Date*   1925
> *Copy*   1925; renewed 1953
> *Parts*   Two editions - SSA and SSAA
> *Loc*   NN, PP, IU
> *Ded*   "To my Mother"

101. *Christmas Candle* (sacred/secular)

> *Text*   Kate Louise Brown
> *Pub*   G. Schirmer, New York
> *Acc*   Piano
> *Date*   1940
> *Copy*   1940; renewed 1968
> *Parts*   Two editions - SA and SSA
> *Solo*   SA edition - Mezzo-soprano

Solo SSA edition - Soprano
Loc NN, PP
Ded "To Jimmy, Wayne, and Elayne"

102. *Christmas Morn* (sacred)

Text 1st and 2nd verses by Grace Widney Mabee;
3rd verse by Agnes Moulton
Pub Harold Flammer, New York
Date 1922
Copy 1922; renewed 1950
Parts SA
Loc NN, PP, LAPL
Note Also published for unison voices

103. *Christ Went Up Into the Hills* (sacred)

Text Katharine Adams
Pub H.W. Gray, New York
Date 1932
Copy 1932; renewed 1960
Parts Two editions - SSA and SSAA
Loc NN, PP
Ded "To Clarence Dickinson"

104. *Come Away* (secular)

Text Margaret Houston
Pub Harold Flammer, New York
Date 1940
Copy 1940
Parts Two editions - SA and SSA
Loc NN, PP

105. *Down In the Glen* (secular)

Text Katharine Adams
Pub G. Schirmer, New York
Date 1931
Copy 1931; renewed 1959
Parts SSA
Loc NN, PP

106. *Fairy Hills of Dream* (secular)

Text Joyce Kilmer

Pub   Harold Flammer, New York
Date   1922
Copy   1922; renewed 1950
Parts   SSA
Loc   NN, PP

107. *Flower Chorus in Spring* (secular)

Text   Anonymous
Pub   John Church, Boston
Date   1922
Copy   1922; renewed 1950
Parts   SSA
Loc   NN, PP, LAPL
Ded   "To The Los Angeles Women's Lyric Club"

108. *The Fountain* (secular)

Text   Sara Teasdale
Pub   G. Schirmer, New York
Date   1937
Copy   1937; renewed 1964
Parts   SSA
Loc   NN, PP

109. *From This Summer Garden* (secular)

Text   Paula Romay
Pub   Carl Fischer, New York
Date   1970
Copy   1970
Parts   SSA
Loc   NN, PP, AWC

110. *Halloween* (secular)

Text   Molly Capes
Pub   Manuscript
Date   1975
Parts   SSA
Loc   NN

111. *The Harp Weaver* (secular) - R

Text   Edna St. Vincent Millay
Pub   Carl Fischer, New York

    Date   1932
    Copy   1932; renewed 1960; 1978
    Parts   SSA
    Solo   Baritone; Optional Harp
    Loc   Carl Fischer, New York (Rental Library);
            NN, PP, CLU

112. *The Heart of Night* (secular)

    Text   Bliss Carman
    Pub   Harold Flammer, New York
    Date   1947
    Copy   1947; renewed 1974
    Parts   SSA
    Loc   NN, PP
    Ded   "To the Women's Lyric Club of Los Angeles"

113. *How to the Singer Comes the Song?* (secular)

    Text   Richard Watson Gilder
    Pub   H.W. Gray, New York
    Date   1930
    Copy   1930; renewed 1957
    Parts   SSAA
    Loc   NN, PP

114. *Hymn to the Night* (secular)

    Text   Henry Wadsworth Longfellow
    Pub   Oliver Ditson, Philadelphia
    Date   1929
    Copy   1928; renewed 1955
    Parts   SSA
    Loc   NN, PP, LAPL

115. *I Hear the Sighing Winds* (secular)

    Text   Austin Harding
    Pub   Galaxy Music, New York
    Date   1947
    Copy   1947; renewed 1974
    Parts   SSA
    Loc   NN, PP

116. *The Little Betrothed* (secular)

     Text   Isabel Hume
     Pub   Carl Fischer, New York
     Date   1936
     Copy   1935; renewed 1963
     Parts   SSA
     Loc   NN, PP

117. *Little Choral Suite* (secular)

    a. *Rain Slippers* - Text: Anonymous
    b. *Sleep Walks Over the Hill* - Text: Rowena Bastin Bennett
    c. *A Little Song of Life* - Text: Lizette Woodworth Reese

     Pub   Carl Fischer, New York
     Date   1973
     Copy   1973
     Parts   SSA
     Loc   Carl Fischer, New York; NN, PP, AWC

118. *Mister Moon* (secular)

     Text   Bliss Carman
     Pub   H.W. Gray, New York
     Date   1933
     Copy   1933; renewed 1961
     Parts   SSA
     Loc   NN, PP
     Ded   "To Rose Coursen Reed and The Treble Clef Club of Portland, Oregon"

119. *Mr. Nobody* (secular)

     Text   Anonymous
     Pub   Galaxy Music. NY
     Date   1947
     Copy   1947; renewed 1975
     Parts   SSA
     Loc   NN, PP

120. *The Night Will Never Stay* (secular)

     Text   Eleanor Farjeon

Pub	Lawson-Gould, New York
Date	1964
Copy	1964
Parts	SSA
Loc	Lawson-Gould, New York; NN, PP, AWC

121. *The Question* (secular)

Text	Katherine Nolen
Pub	H.W. Gray, New York
Date	1941
Copy	1941
Parts	SSA
Loc	NN, PP
Ded	"To the Philomel Singers of Seattle and Mr. R.H. Kendrick, director"

122. *The Sirens* (secular)

Text	James Russell Lowell
Pub	Carl Fischer, New York
Date	1937
Copy	1937; renewed 1964
Parts	SSA
Loc	NN, PP
Ded	"To Antonia Brico and the Treble Clef Chorus of the White Plains Contemporary Club"

123. *Songs for Young Voices* (secular) - R

a. *Sing A Song of Seasons* - Text: Robert Louis Stevenson
b. *Who Has Seen the Wind?* - Text: Christina Rossetti
c. *Boats Sail on the Rivers* - Text: Christina Rossetti
d. *Song of the Clock* - Text: Anonymous
e. *The Swing* - Text: Robert Louis Stevenson
f. *The Falling Star* - Text: Sara Teasdale

Pub	Lawson-Gould, New York
Date	1976
Copy	1976
Parts	SA

> *Loc*   Lawson-Gould, New York; NN, PP, AWC
> *Ded*   "To Zack, Tim, Warren, Kristin, and Nicky"

124. *Spring Morning in the Hills* (from *Four Songs of the Seasons*) (secular)

> *Text*   Mona Modini Wood
> *Pub*   H.W. Gray, New York
> *Date*   1928
> *Copy*   1928; renewed 1956
> *Parts* SSA
> *Loc*   NN, PP

125. *Summer Noon on the Desert* (from "*Four Songs of the Seasons*") (secular)

> *Text*   Mona Modini Wood
> *Pub*   H.W. Gray, New York
> *Date*   1928
> *Copy*   1928; renewed 1956
> *Parts* SSA
> *Loc*   NN, PP

126. *We Are the Music Makers* (secular)

> *Text*   Arthur O'Shaughnessy
> *Pub*   H.W. Gray, New York
> *Date*   1932
> *Copy*   1932; renewed 1960
> *Parts* SSA
> *Loc*   NN, PP
> *Ded*   "Written for and dedicated to the Philomel Singers of Seattle"

127. *White Iris* (secular)

> *Text*   Bliss Carman
> *Pub*   Theodore Presser, Bryn Mawr, PA
> *Date*   1979
> *Copy*   1979
> *Parts* SSA
> *Loc*   Theodore Presser, Bryn Mawr, PA; NN, PP, AWC

128. *Windy Weather* (secular)

Text	James Stephens
Pub	E.C. Schirmer, Boston
Date	1942
Copy	1942; renewed 1969
Parts	SSA
Loc	E.C. Schirmer, Boston; NN, PP, AWCL
Ded	"To the San Francisco Musical Club Choral, and Alfred Hurtgen, Conductor"

129. *Winter Night in the Valley* (from *"Four Songs of the Seasons"*) (secular)

Text	Mona Modini Wood
Pub	H.W. Gray, New York
Date	1928
Copy	1928; renewed 1956
Parts	SSA
Loc	NN, PP

Works for Women's Chorus, a Cappella

130. *Christmas Candle* (sacred/secular)

Text	Kate Louise Brown
Pub	G. Schirmer, New York
Date	1940
Copy	1940; renewed 1968
Parts	SSAA
Solo	Mezzo-Soprano
Loc	NN, PP

131. *Song on May Morning* (secular)

Text	John Milton
Pub	H.W. Gray, New York
Date	1934
Copy	1934; renewed 1962
Parts	SSAA
Loc	NN, PP
Ded	"To Mr. R.H. Kendrick and the Philomel Singers of Seattle, Wash."

Songs for Solo Voice and Piano or Organ (Unless
otherwise stated, accompaniments are for piano.)

132. *Because of Thy Great Bounty* (sacred)

    Text   Grace Noll Crowell
    Pub   H.W. Gray, New York
    Date   1932
    Copy   1932; renewed 1960
    Loc   NN, PP

133. *Blow, Golden Trumpets!* (sacred)

    Text   Margaret Deland
    Pub   Harold Flammer, New York
    Key   High, Low
    Date   1936
    Copy   1936
    Loc   NN, PP, LAPL

134. *By A Fireside* (secular) - R

    Text   Thomas Jones, Jr.
    Pub   G. Schirmer, New York
    Key   High, Low
    Date   1934
    Copy   1934; renewed 1962
    Loc   NN, PP

135. *Caliban in the Coal Mines* (secular)

    Text   Louis Untermeyer
    Pub   Manuscript
    Date   Circa 1950's
    Loc   Composer

136. *Children of the Moon* (secular)

    Text   Katharine Adams
    Pub   Harold Flammer, New York
    Date   1925
    Copy   1925; renewed 1953
    Loc   NN, PP, LAPL
    Ded   "To My Mother"

137. *Christmas Candle* (sacred/secular) - *R*

    Text   Kate Louise Brown
    Pub   Carl Fischer, New York (in *Selected Songs by Elinor Remick Warren*)
    Acc   Also with clarinet obbligato and various flute obbligatos
    Date   1940
    Copy   1940; renewed 1968
    Loc   Carl Fischer, New York (in above collection); NN, PP, AWC, CLU
    Loc   Obbligatos in manuscript: Composer

138. *Christ Went Up Into the Hills* (sacred)

    Text   Katharine Adams
    Pub   H.W. Gray, New York
    Key   High, Low
    Date   1932
    Copy   1932; renewed 1960
    Loc   NN, PP
    Ded   "To Clarence Dickinson"

139. *Come Away!* (secular) - *R*

    Text   Margaret Houston
    Pub   Harold Flammer, New York
    Key   High, Low
    Date   1936
    Copy   1937
    Loc   NN, PP
    Ded   "To Carlotta King"

140. *Down in the Glen* (secular)

    Text   Katharine Adams
    Pub   G. Schirmer, New York
    Date   1931
    Copy   1931; renewed 1959
    Loc   NN, PP

141. *Dreams* (secular)

    Text   Beatrice Fenner
    Pub   Oliver Ditson, Philadelphia
    Key   High, Medium

Date   1927
Copy   1927; renewed 1955
Loc   NN, PP, LAPL, CLSU, OrP

142. *Fairy Hills of Dream* (secular)

Text   Joyce Kilmer
Pub   Harold Flammer, New York
Date   1922
Copy   1922; renewed 1950
Loc   NN, PP, LAPL

143. *Far Hill* (secular)

Text   Francis Carlin
Pub   Galaxy Music, New York
Date   1937
Copy   1937; renewed 1964
Loc   NN, PP

144. *For You With Love* (secular) - *R*

Text   Louis Untermeyer
Pub   G. Schirmer, New York
Acc   Also with optional flute obbligato
Date   1967
Copy   1969
Loc   G. Schirmer, New York; NN, PP, AWC, CLU
Loc   Flute obbligato in manuscript: Composer
Ded   "To Elayne and Tom"

145. *Fulfillment* (secular)

Text   Ross Thompson
Pub   Galaxy Music, New York
Date   1937
Copy   1937; renewed 1964
Loc   NN, PP, CLU

146. *The Glory of His Presence* (sacred)

Text   Joseph Mary Plunkett
Pub   H.W. Gray, New York
Date   1931
Copy   1931; renewed 1959
Loc   NN, PP

147. *God Be in My Heart* (sacred) - R

Text	Anonymous, 16th century
Pub	Oliver Ditson, Philadelphia
Key	High, Medium
Date	1950
Copy	1950; renewed 1978
Loc	NN, PP

148. *God, Our Refuge* (sacred)

Text	From Psalms 18:2, 46:1, 34:4, 85:11, 18:1, 18:28, 143:8
Pub	H.W. Gray, New York
Date	1922
Copy	1922; renewed 1950
Loc	NN, PP, LAPL

149. *Golden Yesterdays* (secular)

Text	Perrin Holmes Lowry
Pub	Harold Flammer, New York
Date	1923
Copy	1923; renewed 1950
Loc	NN, PP, LAPL

150. *Great Memories* (from *Singing Earth*) (secular) - R

Text	Carl Sandburg
Pub	Carl Fischer, New York (in *Selected Songs by Elinor Remick Warren*)
Date	1950
Copy	1950; renewed 1978
Loc	Carl Fischer, New York (in the above collection); NN, PP, AWC

151. *The Heart of a Rose* (secular) - R

Text	Alfred Noyes
Pub	Harold Flammer, New York
Key	High, Low
Date	1922
Copy	1922; renewed 1950
Loc	NN, PP, LAPL
Ded	"To Mme. Margaret Matzenauer"

152. *Heather* (secular) - *R*

    Text   Marguerite Wilkinson
    Pub   Carl Fischer, New York (in *Selected Songs by Elinor Remick Warren*)
    Date   1942
    Copy 1942; renewed 1969
    Loc   Carl Fischer, New York (in the above collection); NN, PP, LAPL, AWC, OrP

153. *Idyll* (sacred)

    Text   Katharine Adams
    Pub   H.W. Gray, New York
    Date   1932
    Copy 1931; renewed 1959
    Loc   NN, PP

154. *If You Have Forgotten* (secular) - *R*

    Text   Sara Teasdale
    Pub   Carl Fischer, New York (in *Selected Songs by Elinor Remick Warren*)
    Date   1940
    Copy 1940; renewed 1968
    Loc   Carl Fischer, New York (in the above collection); NN, PP, AWC, CLU

155. *I Have Seen Dawn* (secular)

    Text   John Masefield
    Pub   Boston Music, Boston
    Date   1924
    Copy 1924; renewed 1952
    Loc   NN, PP, LAPL, FTaSU
    Ded   "To Arthur Kraft"

156. *In a Low Rocking Chair* (secular) - *R*

    Text   Helen Coale Crew
    Pub   Harold Flammer, New York
    Date   1936
    Copy 1936; renewed 1964
    Loc   NN, PP, CLU
    Ded   "For Jimmy"

157. *Invocation to Spring* (secular)

Text	Elizabeth Evelyn Moore
Pub	Harold Flammer, New York
Date	1924
Copy	1924
Loc	NN, PP, LAPL

158. *I Saw A Little Tailor* (secular)

Text	Eleanor Farjeon
Pub	Oliver Ditson Co., Philadelphia
Key	High, Low
Date	1950
Copy	1950; renewed 1978
Loc	NN, PP

159. *King Arthur's Farewell* (from *The Legend of King Arthur*) (secular) - R

Text	Alfred Tennyson
Pub	Carl Fischer, New York
Key	High, Low
Date	1941
Copy	1941; renewed 1969
Loc	Carl Fischer, New York (Rental Library); NN, PP, CLU

160. *Lady Lo-Fu* (formerly *My Lady Lo-Fu*) (secular) - R

Text	Mona Modini Wood
Pub	Carl Fischer, New York (in *Selected Songs by Elinor Remick Warren*)
Acc	Clarinet and various flute obbligatos optional
Date	1927
Copy	1927; renewed 1955
Loc	Carl Fischer, New York (in the above collection); NN, PP, LAPL, AWC, CLSU
Loc	Obbligatos in manuscript: Composer
Ded	"To Florence Easton" (original edition only)

161. *Lament for Love* (secular)

Text	Sydney King Russell

Pub   Carl Fischer, New York
Key   High, Low
Date 1937
Copy 1937; renewed 1964
Loc   NN, PP, CLU

162. *Light the Lamps Up!* (secular) - R

Text Eleanor Farjeon
Pub   G. Schirmer, New York
Key   High, Low
Date 1947
Copy 1947; renewed 1974
Loc   NN, PP, LAPL

163. *The Little Betrothed* (secular) - R

Text Isabel Hume
Pub   Carl Fischer, New York
Key   High, Low
Acc   With optional flute obbligato
Date 1935
Copy 1935; renewed 1963
Loc   NN, PP
Loc   Obbligato in manuscript: Composer
Ded   "To Mme. Lucrezia Bori"

164. *Little Slippers of the Rain* (secular)

Text Ernestine Beyer
Pub   John Church, Boston
Date 1921
Copy 1921
Loc   LAPL, NN

165. *Lonely Roads* (secular) - R

Text John Masefield
Pub   Carl Fischer, New York (in *Selected Songs
        by Elinor Remick Warren*)
Date 1937
Copy 1937; renewed 1964
Loc   Carl Fischer, New York (in above
        collection); NN, PP, AWC, CLU

166. *Love's Riddle* (secular)

Text	Gene Lockhart
Pub	Oliver Ditson, Philadelphia
Key	Medium
Date	1945
Copy	1945; renewed 1972
Loc	NN, PP

167. *Melody Out of My Heart* (secular)

Text	Dorothy Kissling
Pub	Carl Fischer, New York
Key	High, Low
Date	1937
Copy	1937; renewed 1964
Loc	NN, PP
Ded	"To Mme. Grete Stueckgold"

168. *More Things Are Wrought by Prayer* (from *The Legend of King Arthur*) (secular) - R

Text	Alfred Tennyson
Pub	Carl Fischer, New York
Key	High, Low
Acc	Organ
Date	1974
Copy	1974
Loc	Carl Fischer, New York; NN, PP, AWC, CLU

169. *Mr. Nobody* (secular)

Text	Anonymous
Pub	Galaxy Music, New York
Date	1944
Copy	1944; renewed 1972
Loc	NN, PP, CLSU

170. *My Love Is Like a Red Red Rose* (secular)

Text	Robert Burns
Date	1916
Copy	1918
Loc	LAPL
Note	Privately printed for Westlake School, when composer was a student there.

171. *My Parting Gift* (secular) - *R*

    Text   Mrs. Lawrence (Grace) Tibbett
    Pub   Oliver Ditson, Philadelphia
    Key   High, Medium
    Date   1927
    Copy   1927; renewed 1955
    Loc   NN, PP, LAPL, CLSU, OrP, PPCI
    Ded   "To Lawrence Tibbett"

172. *The Nights Remember* (secular) - *R*

    Text   Harold Vinal
    Pub   Carl Fischer, New York
    Key   High, Low
    Date   1937
    Copy   1937; renewed 1964
    Loc   NN, PP

173. *Others!* (secular)

    Text   Anonymous
    Pub   H.W. Gray, New York
    Date   1922
    Copy   1922; renewed 1950
    Loc   NN, PP, LAPL
    Ded   "To Miss Annis Howell"

174. *Piano* (secular) - *R*

    Text   D.H. Lawrence
    Pub   G. Schirmer, New York
    Key   High, Low
    Date   1932
    Copy   1932; renewed 1959
    Loc   NN, PP, CLU
    Ded   "Dedicated to Lawrence Tibbett"

175. *Remembering* (secular)

    Text   Lila Crosby Preston
    Pub   Galaxy Music, New York
    Key   High, Low
    Date   1946
    Copy   1946; renewed 1973

Loc   NN, PP

176. *Sailing Homeward* (secular) - R

Text   Chang Fang-sheng (4th century; trans. by
         Arthur Waley)
Pub   Carl Fischer, New York (in *Selected Songs
         by Elinor Remick Warren*)
Date   1940
Copy   1940; renewed 1968
Loc   Carl Fischer, New York (in above
         collection); NN, PP, AWC, CLU

177. *Silent Noon* (secular) - R

Text   Dante Gabriel Rossetti
Pub   Oliver Ditson, Philadelphia, PA
Key   High, Low
Date   1928
Copy   1928; renewed 1955
Loc   NN, PP, LAPL

178. *Snow Towards Evening* (secular) - R

Text   Melville Cane
Pub   G. Schirmer, New York (in *Songs by 22
         Americans*)
Key   High, Low
Acc   Also with optional flute obbligato
Date   1937
Copy   1937; copyright of collection 1960
Loc   G. Schirmer, New York (in above
         collection); NN, PP, AWC
Loc   Obbligato in manuscript: Composer

179. *A Song of June* (secular)

Text   Bliss Carman
Pub   G. Schirmer, New York
Date   1918
Copy   1919; renewed 1946
Loc   NN, PP, LAPL
Ded   "To Miss Virginia Turner"
Note   This is composer's first published work

180. *Sonnets for Soprano* (secular)

> *Text*   Edna St. Vincent Millay (from *Fatal
> Interview* - Sonnets 7, 11, 35, 52)
> *Pub*   Carl Fischer, NY
> *Date*   1954
> *Copy*   1974
> *Loc*   Carl Fischer, New York (Rental Library);
> NN, PP

181. *Summer Stars* (from *Singing Earth*) (secular) - *R*

> *Text*   Carl Sandburg
> *Pub*   Carl Fischer, New York (in *Selected Songs
> by Elinor Remick Warren*)
> *Date*   1950
> *Copy*   1950; renewed 1978
> *Loc*   Carl Fischer, New York (in above
> collection); NN, PP, AWC

182. *Sweetgrass Range* (secular) - *R*

> *Text*   Edwin Ford Piper
> *Pub*   Carl Fischer, New York
> *Key*   High, Low
> *Date*   1934
> *Copy*   1934; renewed 1962
> *Loc*   NN, PP, OrP, CLU

183. *Tawny Days* (from *Singing Earth*) (secular) - *R*

> *Text*   Carl Sandburg
> *Pub*   Carl Fischer, New York (in *Selected Songs
> by Elinor Remick Warren*)
> *Date*   1950
> *Copy*   1950; renewed 1978
> *Loc*   Carl Fischer, New York (in above
> collection); NN, PP, AWC

184. *Things We Wished* (secular)

> *Text*   Thomas Hardy
> *Pub*   Carl Fischer, New York
> *Key*   High, Low
> *Date*   1937
> *Copy*   1937; renewed 1964

Loc   NN, PP

185. *Through My Open Window* (secular) - *R*

    Text   Mildred Crooks (Mrs. Richard Crooks)
    Pub   G. Schirmer, New York
    Key   High, Low
    Date   1937
    Copy   1937; renewed 1965
    Loc   NN, PP
    Ded   "To Richard Crooks"

186. *Time, You Old Gypsy-Man* (secular)

    Text   Ralph Hodgson
    Pub   Enoch and Sons, New York
    Key   High, Low
    Date   1936
    Copy   1936; renewed 1964
    Loc   NN, PP, LAPL
    Ded   "To Richard Crooks"

187. *To a Blue-Eyed Baby* (secular) - *R*

    Text   Richard Le Gallienne
    Pub   Oliver Ditson, Philadelphia
    Key   High, Low
    Date   1942
    Copy   1950; renewed 1978
    Loc   NN, PP
    Ded   "For Elayne"

188. *To the Farmer* (secular) - *R*

    Text   Inscription on a jug, *Farmer's Arms*
    Pub   Carl Fischer, New York
    Key   High, Medium
    Date   1951
    Copy   1951; renewed 1979
    Loc   NN, PP, OrP
    Ded   "To Nelson Eddy"

189. *The Touch of Spring* (secular)

    Text   Amelia Josephine Burr
    Pub   Enoch and Sons, New York

Key   High, Medium
Date   1922
Copy   1922; renewed 1950
Loc   NN, PP, LAPL
Ded   "To Frank LaForge"

190. *Wander Shoes* (secular) - R

Text   Helen Coale Crew
Pub   Harold Flammer, New York
Key   High, Medium
Date   1936
Copy   1936; renewed 1964
Loc   NN, PP

191. *We Two* (secular) (withdrawn by composer)

Text   Corinna D. Dodge
Pub   Huntzinger, New York
Key   High, Low
Date   1922
Copy   1922

192. *We Two* (secular) - R

Text   Walt Whitman
Pub   G. Schirmer, New York
Key   High, Low
Date   1947
Copy   1947; renewed 1974
Loc   NN, PP, CLU

193. *When You Walk Through Woods* (secular) - R

Text   Leighton G. Harris
Pub   Oliver Ditson Company, Philadelphia
Key   High, Low
Date   1950
Copy   1950; renewed 1978
Loc   NN, PP

194. *White Horses of the Sea* (secular) - R

Text   Hamish Hendry
Pub   Carl Fischer, New York (in *Selected Songs
        by Elinor Remick Warren*)

Date   1932
Copy   1932; renewed 1959
Loc   Carl Fischer, New York (in above
        collection); NN, PP, LAPL, AWC, CLSU,
        CLU
Ded   "Dedicated to Richard Crooks"

195. *Who Calls?* (secular) - R

Text   Frances Clarke Sayers
Pub   Carl Fischer, New York
Key   High, Low
Date   1937
Copy   1937; renewed 1964
Loc   NN, PP
Ded   "To Queena Mario"

196. *Who Loves the Rain* (secular) - R

Text   Frances Shaw
Pub   Carl Fischer, New York (in *Selected Songs
        by Elinor Remick Warren*)
Date   1945
Copy   1945; renewed 1972
Loc   Carl Fischer, New York (in above
        collection); NN, PP, AWC, CLU
Ded   "To Wayne"

197. *The Wind Sings Welcome* (from *Singing Earth*)
(secular) - R

Text   Carl Sandburg
Pub   Carl Fischer, New York (in *Selected Songs
        by Elinor Remick Warren*)
Acc   Piano, with optional flute and clarinet
        obbligato
Date   1950
Copy   1950; renewed 1978
Loc   Carl Fischer, New York (in above
        collection); NN, PP, AWC
Loc   Obbligato in manuscript: Composer

COLLECTIONS (Songs listed in catalog individually by title.)

C-1. *Selected Songs by Elinor Remick Warren*

Pub	Carl Fischer, New York
Date	1982
Copy	1982
Songs	*Sailing Homeward*
	Lady Lo-Fu
	Heather
	If You Have Forgotten
	White Horses of the Sea
	Lonely Roads
	Christmas Candle
	Who Loves the Rain
	Singing Earth (Song Cycle):
	The Wind Sings Welcome
	Summer Stars
	Tawny Days
	Great Memories
Key	High/Medium Voice
Loc	Carl Fischer, New York; NN, PP, AWC, CLU, DLC, PPCI
Ded	"To Wayne"

C-2. *Songs by 22 Americans: A Collection of Songs by Outstanding American Composers* (compiled by Bernard Taylor)

Pub	G. Schirmer, New York
Copy	1960
Song	*Snow Towards Evening*
Loc	G. Schirmer, New York

C-3. *From the Repertoire of Margaret Matzenauer* (A Group of Five Songs)

Pub	Harold Flammer, New York
Copy	1923
Song	*The Heart of a Rose*

C-4. *Your Nelson Eddy Songs*

Pub   Carl Fischer, New York
Copy   1948
Song   *Sweetgrass Range*

DISCOGRAPHY

Commercial Recordings

Elinor Remick Warren, Accompanist and Composer

Cambria Records - Cassette Tape CT-1028; Compact Disc CD-1028

Art Songs by Elinor Remick Warren
Marie Gibson, soprano; Elinor Remick Warren, piano; Catherine Smith, flute

When You Walk Through Woods
God Be In My Heart
Light the Lamps Up!
Silent Noon
The Nights Remember
In a Low Rocking Chair
Who Loves the Rain
We Two
To a Blue-Eyed Baby
Sailing Homeward
If You Have Forgotten
Who Calls?
Heather
By a Fireside
White Horses of the Sea
Piano
Lonely Roads
Lady Lo-Fu
Snow Towards Evening
The Little Betrothed
For You With Love
Christmas Candle
Singing Earth (Song Cycle): *The Wind Sings Welcome; Summer Stars; Tawny Days; Great Memories*

Elinor Remick Warren, Composer

Composers Recordings, Inc. - CRI 172 (LP)
  Abram in Egypt
    Roger Wagner Chorale; London Philharmonic
    Orchestra; Ronald Lewis, baritone; Roger Wagner,
    conductor
  Suite for Orchestra
    Oslo Philharmonic Orchestra; William Strickland,
    conductor

Plymouth Records - Digital LP, Plymouth 91881
  *Anne Perillo Sings Songs by Elinor Remick Warren
  and Other American Composers*
    Anne Perillo, soprano
      Heather
      Who Loves the Rain
      For You With Love
      Great Memories
      Christmas Candle
      When You Walk Through Woods

Daina-Life Records - LP - CF-1684 (A9KB715)
  American Art Songs
    Alden Andreassen, tenor
      Wander Shoes

Presser Recording - LP - EO-LCC-218
  Rose Bampton Sings to You
    Rose Bampton, soprano
      God Be in My Heart

Decca - 78RPM - DLA 2577
  Christmas Candle
    Tony Martin, baritone, and orchestra

Victor Red Seal - 78RPM - 10-1119-A
  Christmas Candle
    John Charles Thomas, baritone

Victor Red Seal - 78RPM - 1979-B
  My Parting Gift
    Frederick Jagel, tenor

Rococco Records - LP - 5292
  Wander Shoes
    Frederick Jagel, tenor

Chime Records - LP - 1005
Christ Is Born
The Earl Snapp Chorale
Christmas Candle

Supreme Records - LP, Stereo - SS-2075
The Best of Christmas
The Paul Mickelson Choir and Orchestra
Christmas Candle

RCA Victor - LP - LPM-1517
The Best of Christmas
Paul Mickelson Orchestra and Choir
Christmas Candle

Zondewan Victory Recording - LP - ZIP-546
Christmas at Quito
Joe Springer
Christmas Candle

Elinor Remick Warren, Pianist

Okeh Records - 78 RPM
40147-A   *The Frolic of the Elves*
               (Elinor Remick Warren)
40147-B   *Dedication* (Schumann-Liszt)
4873-A   *Papillons* (Ole Olson)
4873-B   *Country Dance No. 1* (Beethoven)
40070-A   *Guitarre* (Moszkowski)
40070-B   *Juba* (R. Nathaniel Dett)
40159-A   *Humoreske* (Rachmaninoff)
40159-B   *Rigaudon* (E.A. MacDowell)
73143-A   *Rosamunde Ballet* (Schubert)
73143-B   *Troika* (Tschaikowsky)

Accompaniments from the Art Song Repertoire -
78 RPM (further information unknown)

Non-Commercial Recordings

Records and tapes located in the Fleisher Collection, Free
Library of Philadelphia, and in the Rodgers and Hammer-
stein Archives of Recorded Sound, The New York Public
Library at Lincoln Center.

Included in the list are several commercial recordings
listed above. They are mentioned here also to indicate
their availability for listening at these two archives.

Orchestral

Along the Western Shore (3 movements) (tape)
   Performers   Los Angeles Philharmonic Orchestra,
                    John Barnett, conductor
   Date   October 31, 1954 (premiere
                    performance)
   Performance   *The Standard Hour* - NBC Radio
                    (broadcast to schools only)

The Crystal Lake (tape)
   Performers   Los Angeles Philharmonic Orchestra,
                    Alfred Wallenstein, conductor
   Date   March 21, 1946 (premiere
                    performance)
   Performance   Concert, Philharmonic Auditorium, Los
                    Angeles

Suite for Orchestra (4 movements) (CRI-172)
   Performers   Oslo Philharmonic, William Strickland,
                    conductor

Symphony in One Movement (tape)
   Performers   Los Angeles Philharmonic Orchestra,
                    Gerhard Samuel, conductor
   Date   May 26, 1972
   Performance   Concert, Royce Hall, UCLA

Intermezzo (from *The Legend of King Arthur*) (tape)
   Performers   Sinfonia Orchestra, Roger Wagner,
                    conductor
   Date   January 30, 1971
   Performance   From performance of the full work,
                    Dorothy Chandler Pavilion, Music
                    Center, Los Angeles

The Fountain (tape)
Performers	San Diego Symphony, Fabien Savitzky, conductor
Date	August 7, 1952
Performance	Concert, San Diego, California

Scherzo (tape)
Performers	WGN Symphony of the Air, Henry Weber, conductor
Date	November 14, 1951
Performance	WGN Radio, Chicago, Illinois

Orchestra with Soloist

Sonnets for Soprano and String Quartet (tape)
Performers	Bonnie Murray and Musart String Quartet
Date	November 14, 1954
Performance	Concert at California Institute of Technology

Singing Earth (orchestral version) (tape)
Performers	Brico Orchestra, Antonia Brico, conductor; soloist: Ellen McLain, soprano
Date	October 19, 1979
Performance	Concert, Denver, Colorado

Sir Bedivere's Lament (aria from *The Legend of King Arthur*) (tape, included on *Seven Songs by Elinor Remick Warren* tape)
Performers	William Olvis, tenor; Sinfonia Orchestra, Roger Wagner, conductor
Date	April 2, 1954
Performance	From performance of full work, Philharmonic Auditorium, Los Angeles

Chorus and Orchestra

Abram in Egypt (LP, CRI-172)
Performers	London Philharmonic, Roger Wagner, conductor; soloist: Ronald Lewis, baritone; Roger Wagner Chorale

Good Morning, America! (tape)

Performers	Honolulu Symphony Orchestra and Chorus, Robert LaMarchina, conductor; narrator: Efrem Zimbalist, Jr.
Date	December 16, 1977
Performance	Concert in Honolulu, Hawaii

Requiem (tape)

Performers	Los Angeles Master Chorale & Sinfonia Orchestra, Roger Wagner, conductor; soloists: Carol Neblett, soprano, Paul Hinshaw, baritone
Date	April 3, 1966 (premiere performance)
Performance	Concert at Dorothy Chandler Pavilion, Los Angeles

The Harp Weaver (tape)

Performers	Women of the Los Angeles Master Chorale, Roger Wagner, conductor, with baritone, harp and piano
Date	February 15, 1969
Performance	Concert at Statham House, Los Angeles

The Legend of King Arthur (1974 revision) (tape)

Performers	Los Angeles Master Chorale & Sinfonia Orchestra, Roger Wagner, conductor; soloists: William Chapman, baritone, George Metcalfe, tenor
Date	January 30, 1971
Performance	Concert at Dorothy Chandler Pavilion, Music Center, Los Angeles

Transcontinental (tape)

Performers	Occidental College Orchestra and Chorus, Howard Swan, conductor
Date	May 26, 1958 (premiere performance)
Performance	Concert at Occidental College

Voice and Piano

To the Children and *In a Low Rocking Chair* (tape)

Performers	Delphine Fahringer, soprano; piano accompaniment by Elinor Remick Warren
Songs	*A Summer Morning* *Cloud Sheep* *The Apple Song* *Mr. Frisky-Squirrel* *Sing a Song of Seasons* *Who Has Seen the Wind?* *Boats Sail on the Rivers* *The Clock* *The Swing* *Falling Star* *The Little Plant*
Performance	Studio recording (Some of these songs are solo versions of Warren's choral work for SA, *Songs For Young Voices*)
Song	*In a Low Rocking Chair*
Performer	Carlotta King, soprano
Performance	Studio recording

Singing Earth (piano-vocal of orchestral song cycle) (tape included on reverse of *Seven Songs by Elinor Remick Warren* tape)

Performers	Joyce Sweeney, soprano; piano accompaniment by Elinor Remick Warren
Date	February 2, 1979
Performance	Concert, MacDowell Club of Los Angeles

Seven Songs by Elinor Remick Warren (tape)

Song	*King Arthur's Farewell* (aria from *The Legend of King Arthur*)
Performers	James O'Neil, tenor; piano accompaniment by Elinor Remick Warren
Date	February 2, 1979
Performance	Concert, MacDowell Club of Los Angeles

Song	*Sir Bedivere's Lament* (aria from *The Legend of King Arthur*)
Performers	William Olvis, tenor; Sinfonia Orchestra, Roger Wagner, conductor
Date	April 2, 1954
Performance	Performance of full work, Philharmonic Auditorium, Los Angeles
Song	*If You Have Forgotten*
Performers	Joyce Sweeney, soprano; piano accompaniment by Elinor Remick Warren
Date	February 2, 1979
Performance	Concert, MacDowell Club of Los Angeles
Song	*Lady Lo-Fu*
Performers	Joyce Sweeney, soprano; piano accompaniment by Elinor Remick Warren
Date	February 2, 1979
Performance	Concert, MacDowell Club of Los Angeles
Song	*To the Farmer*
Performers	James O'Neil, tenor; piano accompaniment by Elinor Remick Warren
Date	February 2, 1979
Performance	Concert, MacDowell Club of Los Angeles
Song	*Snow Towards Evening*
Performers	Joyce Sweeney, soprano; piano accompaniment by Elinor Remick Warren
Date	February 2, 1979
Performance	Concert, MacDowell Club of Los Angeles
Song	*We Two*
Performers	Joyce Sweeney, soprano; piano accompaniment by Elinor Remick Warren
Date	February 2, 1979

Performance	Concert, MacDowell Club of Los Angeles

Twenty-two Songs by Elinor Remick Warren (tape)

Song	*The Heart of a Rose*
Performers	Theresa Stitch-Randall, soprano; piano accompaniment by Elinor Remick Warren
Performance	Studio recording
Song	*When You Walk Through Woods*
Performers	Theresa Stitch-Randall, soprano; piano accompaniment by Elinor Remick Warren
Performance	Studio recording
Song	*To a Blue-Eyed Baby*
Performers	Cora Lauridson, contralto; piano accompaniment by Elinor Remick Warren
Performance	Studio recording
Song	*Christmas Candle*
Performer	Richard Crooks, tenor, with orchestra
Date	December 6, 1943
Performance	*Voice of Firestone* radio program
Song	*More Things Are Wrought by Prayer* (aria from *The Legend of King Arthur*)
Performer	Patricia Beems, soprano, with organ
Performance	Church recording
Song	*My Parting Gift* (commercial recording)
Performer	Frederick Jagel, tenor, with piano accompaniment by Edwin McArthur
Recording	RCA Victor recording 1979-B
Song	*Come Away*
Performers	Lee Sweetland, baritone; piano accompaniment by Elinor Remick Warren
Performance	Studio recording
Song	*The Wind Sings Welcome* (from song cycle *Singing Earth*)

Performers	Theresa Stitch-Randall, soprano; piano accompaniment by Elinor Remick Warren
Performance	Studio recording
Song	*Summer Stars* (from song cycle *Singing Earth*)
Performers	Theresa Stitch-Randall, soprano; piano accompaniment by Elinor Remick Warren
Performance	Studio recording
Song	*Tawny Days* (from song cycle *Singing Earth*)
Performers	Theresa Stitch-Randall, soprano; piano accompaniment by Elinor Remick Warren
Performance	Studio recording
Song	*Great Memories* (from song cycle *Singing Earth*)
Performers	Raymond Manton, tenor; Los Angeles Philharmonic, Carmen Dragon, conductor
Date	June 9, 1959
Performance	*The Standard Hour* - NBC Radio
Song	*For You with Love*
Performer	Richard Crooks, tenor, wtih organ
Date	April 8, 1967 (first performance)
Performance	Wilshire Methodist Church, Los Angeles (at wedding of composer's daughter)
Song	*Wander Shoes*
Performers	Lee Sweetland, baritone; piano accompaniment by Elinor Remick Warren
Performance	Studio recording
Song	*Who Calls?*
Performers	Ruth Felt, soprano; piano accompaniment by Elinor Remick Warren
Performance	*American Composers* program, Mutual Broadcasting System

Song	*By a Fireside*
Performers	Ruth Felt, soprano, with orchestra
Performance	*American Composers* program, Mutual Broadcasting System
Song	*Sailing Homeward*
Performer	Richard Crooks, tenor, with orchestra
Date	December 9, 1940
Performance	*Voice of Firestone* radio program
Song	*Through My Open Window*
Perfomers	Richard Crooks, tenor; piano accompaniment by Elinor Remick Warren
Performance	Home recording
Song	*God Be in My Heart* (commercial recording)
Performer	Rose Bampton, soprano, with piano
Recording	*Rose Bampton Sings to You* - Theodore Presser LP (EO-LCC-218)
Song	*Heather*
Performers	Lee Sweetland, baritone; piano accompaniment by Elinor Remick Warren
Performance	Studio recording
Song	*Lonely Roads*
Performers	Cora Lauridson, contralto; piano accompaniment by Elinor Remick Warren
Performance	Studio recording
Song	*Sweetgrass Range*
Performer	Nelson Eddy, baritone, with orchestra
Date	August 26, 1948
Performance	*Kraft Music Hall* radio program
Song	*White Horses of the Sea*
Performer	Raymond Manton, tenor, with piano
Performance	*The Standard Hour* - NBC Radio

Solo Instrumental

Processional March (tape, on reverse of *Seven Songs by Elinor Remick Warren* tape)

Performer	Ruth Plummer, organ
Date	April 8, 1967
Performance	Wilshire Methodist Church, Los Angeles (as played at the wedding of the composer's daughter)

Air Checks

During radio's heyday, there were numerous classical musical concerts programmed weekly on national networks. Many of Elinor Remick Warren's songs were sung on these programs by leading concert artists. The following is only a partial list of air checks of some of these programs:

1/26/33	Program unknown *The Fountain*; Elinor Remick Warren, piano soloist in her own composition
2/26/35	*Packard Program* *Sweetgrass Range*; Lawrence Tibbett
6/6/37	*Chevrolet Program* *Remembering*; Marion Claire
12/18/38	*The Harp Weaver* Don Lee Broadcasting System
3/21/40	*The Passing of King Arthur* (premiere performance); Los Angeles Philharmonic and Los Angeles Oratorio Society, Paul Keast, baritone, David Laughlin, tenor, Albert Coates, conductor Mutual Broadcasting System
3/24/40	International hookup, via CBS *Arise My Heart and Sing*; Helen Jepson & Chorus; Elinor Remick Warren, accompanist Presented from Forest Lawn - Easter Sunrise Service

9/1/40	*Ford Sunday Evening Hour* *Through My Open Window*; Jimmy Newell & the Ford Orchestra
12/9/40	*Voice of Firestone* *Sailing Homeward*; Richard Crooks
12/22/40	*Ford Sunday Evening Hour* (1) *Christmas Candle* (2) *White Horses of the Sea* both sung by Richard Crooks
12/22/40	CBS *Christmas Candle*; John Charles Thomas
6/21/41	KHJ, Los Angeles *The Question*; Philomel Singers of Seattle
11/3/41	NBC *Through My Open Window*; Lee Sweetland
11/4/41	NBC *Wander Shoes*; Lee Sweetland
11/5/41	NBC *White Horses of the Sea*; Lee Sweetland
1/15/42	*The Standard Hour* *Dark Hills* from *Along the Western* *Shore*; Standard Symphony
2/19/42	NBC *By a Fireside*; Lee Sweetland
2/23/42	NBC *Through My Open Window*; Lee Sweetland
4/27/42	NBC *Wander Shoes*; Lee Sweetland
12/6/43	*Voice of Firestone* *Christmas Candle*; Richard Crooks
7/7/47	*Bell Telephone Hour* *Sweetgrass Range*; Lee Sweetland

8/26/48	*Kraft Music Hall* *Sweetgrass Range*; Nelson Eddy
12/20/48	*Bell Telephone Hour* *Christmas Candle*; John Charles Thomas
11/14/51	*WGN Symphony of the Air* (Chicago) *Scherzo*; WGN Symphony Orchestra, Henry Weber, conductor
5/17/53	*NBC Symphony* *The Crystal Lake*; NBC Symphony Orchestra, Wilfrid Pelletier, conductor
5/16/54	*The Standard Hour* *The Fountain*; Standard Symphony, John Barnett, conductor
10/31/54	*The Standard Hour* *Along the Western Shore*; Standard Symphony, John Barnett, conductor
1/23/55	ABC Radio Paulena Carter with Elinor Remick Warren
6/9/59	Standard School Broadcast (1) *Crystal Lake* (2) *Singing Earth: Great Memories* (3) *White Horses of the Sea* Los Angeles Philharmonic, Carmen Dragon, conductor, Raymond Manton, tenor
Date Unknown	Program Unknown *Christmas Candle*; Rose Bampton (with orchestra)
Date Unknown	*Westinghouse Program* *Heather*; John Charles Thomas
Date Unknown	Mutual Broadcasting System *American Composers* *The Fountain*; Frederick Stark and Orchestra

Date *Unknown*	Mutual Broadcasting System *American Composers* (1) *By a Fireside*; Ruth Felt and Orchestra (2) *Who Calls?*; Ruth Felt, accompanied by Elinor Remick Warren
Date *Unknown*	*The Standard Hour* *White Horses of the Sea*; Raymond Manton
Date *Unknown*	*The Standard Hour* *Suite for Orchestra: Black Cloud Horses*; *Cloud Peaks* Standard Symphony, John Barnett, conductor

AUTHORS OF TEXTS USED IN
WARREN COMPOSITIONS

Numbers following each name refer to works as listed in catalog.

Adams, Katherine; 10, 48, 71, 100, 103, 105, 136, 138, 140, 153
Anonymous; 107
Anonymous; 117
Anonymous; 119
Anonymous; 123
Anonymous; 16th century, 75, 147
Anonymous; 119, 169
Anonymous; 173

Bennett, Rowena Bastin; 117
Beyer, Ernestine; 164
Blake, William; 25, 62
Bonner, Samuel; 26, 63
Book of Common Prayer; 64, 79
Brooks, Phillips; 73
Brown, Kate Louise; 9, 46, 72, 87, 101, 123, 130, 137
Bryant, William Cullen; 54
Burns, Robert; 170
Burr, Amelia Josephine; 189
Byrom, John; 64, 79

Cane, Melville; 178
Capes, Molly; 108
Carlin, Francis; 143
Carman, Bliss; 76, 112, 118, 127, 179
Cawood, Rev. John; 52
Chang, Fang-sheng (trans. by Arthur Waley); 176
Chaucer, Geoffrey; 24, 61
Collect (ancient); 64, 79
Crew, Helen Coale; 156, 190
Crooks, Mildred (Mrs. Richard); 185

INDEX OF FIRST LINES

Numbers following each line refer to works as listed in catalog.

But now, farewell, I am going a long way; 13, 159

Christ went up into the hills alone,/Walking slowly the
    winding way; 48, 103, 138
Christians Awake! Salute the happy morn! 64, 79
Clearly my ruined garden as it stood/Before the frost
    came on it I recall--; 18, 33, 180
Cliffs that rise a thousand feet/Without a break; 176
Clover nods, the bees are loud, as drowsily content I lie,
    The; 149
Come sell your pony, cowboy,/Sell your pony to me; 91,
    182
Come to the stable where Jesus is lying, Born in a manger
    the Saviour and King; 49

Day of anger, day of wrath; 27
Did you ever lie in some grassy spot; 121
Down in the glen, through the silence of the
    leaves,/Listen! 10, 105, 140
Do you fear the force, the force of the wind; 97
Dreams of a mystic seashore,/Where the sands are
    glistening white; 11, 141

Ev'ry little house I see/Underneath its vine and
    tree/Wakes a wistfulness in me; 104, 139
Ev'rywhere, ev'rywhere, Christmas tonight! 73

From glory unto glory! Be this our joyous song; 50

Glad that I live am I,/That the sky is blue; 117
God be in my head/And in my understanding; 75, 147
God, we don't like to complain, we know that the mine is
    no lark--; 135
Grant them rest eternal, O Lord, forevermore; 27
Grant them rest eternal, rest eternal grant unto them; 27
Grip of the ice is gone now, The; 17, 197

Heart once broken is a heart no more, The; 18, 33, 180
Heaven is a fine place, a fine place entirely; 156
He travels far from other skies; 29
High up, just seen/The topmost palace spire; 29
Holy, Holy, Holy Lord God, Lord God of Sabaoth; 27, 28,
    65

During 1938 and 1939, Elinor Remick Warren appeared on the Mutual-Don Lee Networks in a weekly series of Sunday afternoon programs where she spoke about music and played piano selections. The following is a list of the music she played and the composers she discussed during this season of radio programs.

October 30, 1938
Aufswang	Schumann
The Happy Spirits	Gluck
Two Preludes	Arensky

November 13
Prelude in E Minor	Mendelssohn
Nocturne in F Sharp Major	Chopin
Sevillanas	Albeniz

November 20
Organ Prelude in G Minor	Bach
Jesu, Joy of Man's Desiring	Bach
Prelude in A Minor	Debussy

November 27
The Fountain	Elinor Remick Warren
Scherzo in C Sharp Minor	Chopin

December 4
Ballade, "Edward"	Brahms
Little Girls in the Garden	Mompou
Polonaise	MacDowell

December 11
Romance	Schumann
Frolic of the Elves	Elinor Remick Warren
Impromptu in F Sharp Major	Chopin

December 18
The Harp Weaver	Elinor Remick Warren

January 1, 1939
 Troika   Tschaikowsky
 Intermezzo (*Lullaby*)   Brahms
 Cracovienne Fantastique   Paderewski

January 8
 Praeludium   MacDowell
 Nocturne in D Flat Major   Chopin
 Sequidillas   Albeniz

January 15
 To the Sea   MacDowell
 Alceste Caprice   Gluck/Saint-Saëns

January 22
 If Thou Art Near   Bach/Warren
 Rhapsody in B Minor   Brahms
 Butterflies   Olsen

January 29
 Second Ballade in F Major   Chopin
 Tango Americain   Carpenter

February 5
 Country Dance No. 1   Beethoven
 The Sunken Cathedral   Debussy
 Dedication   Schumann/Liszt

February 12
 Bourrée   Handel
 Romance   LaForge
 Spinning Girls of Carentec   Rhenê-Baton

February 19
 Eight Scenes from Childhood   Schumann
 Grande Valse in A Flat   Chopin

February 26
 Prelude   Schütt
 Meditation   Tschaikowsky
 Gavotte   Gluck
 Ragamuffin   Ireland

March 5
 Rigadon   MacDowell
 Nocturne in E Major   Chopin
 Etude Héroïque   Leschetizsky

BIBLIOGRAPHY

Primary Sources

Interviews with Warren, her family, friends, and colleagues
Letters to and from Elinor Remick Warren
Elinor Remick Warren Scrapbooks: 1935 to present
Z. Wayne Griffin Scrapbook
Privately published Warren Family History
Various family collections: wedding and baby books; diary of children's sayings, trip books, etc.
Warren scores, published and unpublished manuscripts
Commercial recordings, private and family recordings, air checks
Photographs and photo albums
Warren program notes and notes for speeches
Copyright data
Scripts for Elinor Remick Warren network radio series
Westlake School Yearbook, 1918
Miscellaneous memorabilia: programs, awards, citations, etc.

Secondary Sources

Books and Reference Works

Ammer, Christine. *Unsung: A History of Women in American Music.* Westport, CT: Greenwood Press, 1980.
Anderson, Ruth E. *Contemporary American Composers: A Biographical Dictionary.* Boston: G.K. Hall, 1976.
ASCAP Biographical Dictionary of Composers, Authors, and Publishers. New York & London: R.R. Bowker, 1980.

Baker, Theodore. *Baker's Biographical Dictionary of Musicians.* 7th ed. Nicolas Slonimsky, ed. New York: Schirmer Books, 1984.

Barnes, Edwin Ninyon Chaloner. *American Women in Creative Music.* Washington, DC: Music Education Publications, 1936.

Barrett, Henry. *The Viola: Complete Guide for Teachers and Students.* University, AL: University of Alabama Press, 1972.

Block, A.F., & C. Neuls-Bates. *Women in American Music: A Bibliography of Music & Literature.* Westport, CT: Greenwood Press, 1979.

Bohle, Bruce, ed. *The International Cyclopedia of Music & Musicians,* 10th ed. London: Dent, 1975.

Bowers, Jane, & Judith Tick, eds. *Women Making Music: The Western Art Tradition, 1150-1950.* Champaign-Urbana, IL: University of Illinois Press, 1986.

Bull, Storm. *Index to Biographies of Contemporary Composers.* Metuchen, NJ: Scarecrow Press, 1964.

Butterworth, Neil. *A Dictionary of American Composers.* New York: Garland Press, 1984.

Cohen, Aaron I., ed. *International Encyclopedia of Women Composers.* New York & London: R.R. Bowker, 1981.
____. *International Discography of Women Composers.* Westport, CT: Greenwood Press, 1984.

Dictionary of International Biography. Cambridge: Melrose Press, 1984.

Dox, Thurston J., comp. *American Oratorios and Cantatas: A Catalog of Works Written in the United States from Colonial Times to 1985.* Metuchen, NJ: Scarecrow Press, 1986.

Eagon, Angelo. *Catalog of Published Concert Music By American Composers.* Metuchen, NJ: Scarecrow Press, 1969. Supplement, 1974.

Edwin A. Fleisher Collection of Orchestral Music in the Free Library of Philadelphia: A Cumulative Catalogue, 1929-1977. Boston: G.K. Hall, 1979.

Etude Historical Musical Portrait Series. Etude: January 1932-October 1940.

Finell, Judith Greenberg. *American Music Center Library Catalogue of Choral and Vocal Works.* New York: American Music Center Library, 1975.

Finger, Susan Pearl. *Women Composers in Los Angeles: 1918-1939.* Doctoral Dissertation. UCLA, 1986.

Frasier, Jane. *Women Composers: A Discography.* Detroit Studies in Music, 1983.

Hitchcock, H. Wiley, & Stanley Sadie, eds. *The New Grove Dictionary of American Music.* New York: Macmillan, 1986.

Hixon, D.L. & Don Hennessee. *Women in Music: A Biobibliography.* Metuchen, NJ & London: Scarecrow Press, 1975.

International Encyclopedia of Women Composers. New York: R.R. Bowker, 1981.

International Who's Who in Music. Cambridge: Melrose Press, 1975.

International Who's Who in Music. London: Melrose Press, 1984.

Ireland, Norma Olin. *Index to Women of the World from Ancient to Modern Times.* Westwood, MA: F.W. Faxon, 1970.

Lawrence, Mary. *Lovers.* New York: Balance House, 1982. [includes an entry by Warren]

LePage, Jane Weiner. *Women Composers, Conductors and Musicians of the 20th Century.* Metuchen, NJ & London: Scarecrow Press, 1983.

Lerner, Ellen. *The Music of Selected Contemporary American Women Composers: A Stylistic Analysis.* Amherst, MA: University of Massachusetts, 1978.

Macmillan Encyclopaedia of Music and Musicians. London: Macmillan, 1938.

Mannheimer Musiktage: Internationalen Wettbewerb für Komponistinnen. Mannheim: Mannheim-Ludwigshafen N.P., 1961.

McArthur, Edwin. *Flagstad: A Personal Memoir.* New York: Alfred A. Knopf, 1965.

McCoy, Guy. *Portraits of the World's Best Women Musicians.* Philadelphia: Presser, 1946.

Oja, Carol J., ed. *American Music Recordings: A Discography of 20th Century U.S. Composers.* New York: Brooklyn College Conservatory, 1982.

Smith, Julia, ed. *Directory of American Women Composers.* Chicago: National Federation of Music Clubs, 1970.
Stern, Susan. *Women Composers: A Handbook.* Metuchen, NJ: Scarecrow Press, 1978.
Stewart-Green, Miriam. *Women Composers: A Checklist of Works for the Solo Voice.* Boston: G.K. Hall, 1980.
Swan, Howard. *Music in the Southwest.* Pasadena, CA: Huntington Library, 1952.

Who's Who in American Music. New York & London: R.R. Bowker, 1983.
Who's Who in Music and Musicians' International Directory, 5th ed. New York: Hafner, 1969.
World Who's Who of Women. London: Melrose Press, 1973.

Zaimont, Judith Lang, & Karen Famera, comps. *Contemporary Concert Music by Women: A Directory of the Composers and Their Works.* Vol. I. Westport, CT: Greenwood Press, 1981.

Articles:
Newspapers, Periodicals, Album Notes (Selected List)

"A Happy Blend," *Musical Courier* (February 15, 1955), cover photo & p. 7.
"*Abram in Egypt* and *Suite for Orchestra* by Elinor Remick Warren." Album notes, CRI LP 172.
"*Abram in Egypt:* Warren International Festival Premiere," Sigma Alpha Iota *Pan Pipes* (January 1962).
"American Composer Update," Sigma Alpha Iota *Pan Pipes* (Winter, 1980). With portrait.
"American Composer Update: The 1982 Premieres, Performances, Publications, Recordings, News," Sigma Alpha Iota *Pan Pipes* (Winter, 1983).
"Another World Premiere," *Pacific Coast Musician* (March 16, 1940).

Argadinos, B. "A Concert by the State Orchestra with American Works," *Avghi* (July 30, 1955). Review of *Singing Earth* in Athens, Greece.

Arlen, Walter. "Master Chorale at Pavilion," *Los Angeles Times* (February 1, 1971). Review of 1971 performance of *The Passing of King Arthur*.

_____. "Nan Merriman Heard in Brilliant Recital," *Los Angeles Times* (October 10, 1960). Review includes *If You Have Forgotten*.

Armistead, Mary B. "Women Will Make Mark in Music, Symphony's Visiting Composer Says," *The World News* [Roanoke, VA] (May 1, 1972).

"Barbirolli's Conducting Wins Praise," *Los Angeles Examiner* (August 9, 1941). Review of *Intermezzo* from *The Passing of King Arthur*.

Barnett, Muriel. "Philharmonic Will Premiere Feminine Composer's *Suite*," *Mirror-News* [Los Angeles] (February 28, 1955).

Beaver, J. Kenneth. "Symphony in Colorful Concert; Soloist Pleases," *The Patriot* [Harrisburg, PA] (November 21, 1951). Review of *Sea Rhapsody* from *Along the Western Shore*.

Bernheimer, Martin. "Chorale's Program Stimulating," *Los Angeles Times* (April 4, 1966). Review of *Requiem*.

Biggs, Gloria. "Californian Links Composer and Homemaker Roles While Cheerfully Rejecting Concert-Stage Career," *Christian Science Monitor* (February 20, 1952).

"Bowl Audience Larger Than Usual at Quartet, Soprano, Pianist Concert," [newspaper unidentified] (August 3, 1960). Review of *Sonnets for Soprano and String Quartet*.

Bronson, Carl. "Acclaim Miss Warren's New Symphonic Poem," *Los Angeles Evening Herald and Express* (March 22, 1940). Review of premiere of *The Passing of King Arthur*.

_____. "American Composer's Symphonic Poem Premiere Set," *Los Angeles Evening Herald and Express* (March 16, 1940).

_____. "Elite Enthuse at Composers' Music Fete," *Los Angeles Herald-Express* (May 26, 1937). Review of *Quintet for Woodwinds*.

____. "Flagstad in Triumph at Recital," *Los Angeles Herald-Express* (May 4, 1938). Review of Flagstad's singing of *Snow Towards Evening*.

____. "Richard Crooks Scores Triumph in Concert," *Los Angeles Evening Herald and Express* (April 12, 1939). Review of songs by Warren performed in this recital.

____. "Sigma Alpha Iota Musicians Charm L.A. Audiences," *Los Angeles Herald-Express* (August 11, 1941). Review of *The Harp Weaver*.

____. "Symphony Charms," *Los Angeles Herald-Examiner* (March 22, 1946). Review of *The Crystal Lake*.

Brown, Ray C.B. "Crooks and Kindler Score in Constitution Hall Concert," *The Washington Post* (November 27, 1941). Review of premiere of *King Arthur's Farewell* from *The Passing of King Arthur*.

Bryant, Marshall F. "Symphony Orchestra Gives Excellent Concert," *Portland* [Maine] *Press Herald* (April 14, 1965). Review of *The Crystal Lake*.

Burk, Gay. "Woman Composer Wins High Praise from Career-Approving Husband," *Honolulu Star-Bulletin* (July 21, 1952).

Callin, Owen. "Fine Concert Given by Pair," *Los Angeles Herald and Express* (August 6, 1952). Review of *The Crystal Lake*.

Cariaga, Daniel. "Composers in the Spotlight," *Los Angeles Times* (November 27, 1977).

____. "Glendale Symphony Praised; L.A. Chorale Event Under Par," *Long Beach* [CA] *Independent* (April 5, 1966). Review criticizing L.A. Master Chorale's singing and interpretation of *Requiem* in its premiere.

Carr, Jay. "Kostelanetz Leads Classic Program in Kresge Concert," *Detroit News* (February 11, 1974). Review of *The Crystal Lake*.

Cavin, Patty. "Washington Is Music to the Griffins' Ears," *Washington Post* (June 26, 1954).

"Composer Extraordinary: Elinor Remick Warren," National Federation of Music Clubs *Music Clubs Magazine* (Summer, 1984).

"Composer Praises Feld Quartet, Bowl Audience." Newspaper unidentified (August 3, 1960).

"Concerts of the State Orchestra: Works by American Composers," *Nea Estia* [Athens, Greece] (August 15, 1955). Review of *Singing Earth* in Athens.

"Concert Features Piece by Elinor R. Warren," *The Chronicle* [Los Angeles] (August, 1976). About *Abram in Egypt* in Israel.

Cook, J. Douglas. "Visits to the Homes of Famous Composers No. XI: Elinor Remick Warren," *Opera and Concert* (March, 1948), 12-13.

Crain, Hal D. "Coates Conducts New Warren Work," *Musical America* (April 5, 1940). Review of premiere of *The Passing of King Arthur.*

Damon, Annabel. "Talented Griffin Family Enjoying Hawaii Visit," Unidentified newspaper (July, 1952).

Donaldson, Herbert. "Composer Parley Lively," *Los Angeles Examiner* (June 8, 1961). Re: panel of composers, in which Warren participated, at L.A. International Music Festival.

_____. "Junior Symphony Stars Two Youths," *Los Angeles Examiner* (November 18, 1961). Review of *The Fountain.*

_____. "L.A. Audience Thrilled by Beverly Orchestra," *Los Angeles Examiner* (May 1, 1961). Review of *Suite for Orchestra.*

Dounias, Min. "Andreas Parides Conducts Works by American Composers," Unidentified Athens, Greece, newspaper (August 15, 1955). Review of *Singing Earth* in Athens.

Downes, Olin. "Women's Ensemble Concludes Season," *New York Times* (April 15, 1936). Review of *The Harp Weaver.*

Driscoll, Marjorie. "Impressive Rite Inspires Throng," *Los Angeles Examiner* (March 25, 1940). Re: Helen Jepson and Glendale Community Chorus, accompanied by Warren, singing *Arise, My Heart, and Sing!* at Forest Lawn Easter Sunrise Service.

Duntley, Louise. "Two Lives: Motherhood, Music," *Los Angeles Examiner* (January 20, 1957).

Eaton, Quaintance. "Women Composers Honored," National
    Federation of Music Clubs *Music Clubs Magazine*
    (April, 1969). Covers New York Public Library exhibit
    and WNYC Radio Festival of American Music.
"Efrem Zimbalist, Jr., Narrates the Symphonic Premiere,"
    Symphony News (June, 1977). With portrait.
"Elinor [Remick] Warren," *Musical Courier* (March 15,
    1952).
"Elinor Remick Warren: Composer Visits P.A. [Palo Alto,
    CA], Sees Music 'Upswing,'" *San Francisco Mercury*
    (July 28, 1961).
"Elinor Remick Warren Has Busy Musical Life," *Musical
    Courier* (June, 1953).
"Elinor Remick Warren Honored in Israel," National Feder-
    ation of Music Clubs *Music Clubs Magazine* (June,
    1977).
"Elinor Remick Warren on Festival Panel," *Santa Monica*
    [CA] *Evening Outlook* (May 26, 1961).
"Elinor Remick Warren Returns from Europe," *Musical
    America* (July, 1953).
"Elinor Remick Warren Work Performed in Hawaii," Na-
    tional Federation of Music Clubs *Music Clubs Maga-
    zine* (Spring, 1978). With portrait.
"Elinor Remick Warren's Activities," *Musical Courier*
    (November 21, 1936).
Elinor Remick Warren's season of 1936-37, *Pacific Coast
    Musician* (date unknown).
"Enjoyable Program at Bowl," *Redlands* [CA] *Daily Facts*
    (September 5, 1945). Review of Warren concert at
    Redlands Bowl, where she appeared both as piano
    soloist and accompanist.
Ennis, Bayard F. "Woman Composer Inspired by West," *The
    Charleston* [WV] *Gazette* (October 24, 1955).
"Exhibition: Contemporary Women Composers in the U.S.,"
    Musical America (August 8, 1963).

Fisher, Marjory M. "Quintet Scores Triumph in New Se-
    ries," *San Francisco News* (January 23, 1940). Review
    of *Quintet for Woodwinds* in its recital debut.
"Five Woman Composers Score in New York City Concert,"
    Danbury [CT] *News Times* (April, 1969).
"Four Works by American Composers," *Nea Estia* [Athens,
    Greece] (July 29, 1955). Review of *Singing Earth*.

Fox, Christy. "Musical Tribute to a Lady," *Los Angeles Times* (October 22, 1967). Story about Warren attending 80th birthday celebration for Nadia Boulanger.

Freund, Bob. "Woman Composer to Be in Audience," unidentified newspaper, Ft. Lauderdale, FL (date unknown).

Goldberg, Albert. "British and French Works Performed," *Los Angeles Times* (June 9, 1961). Review of world premiere of *Abram in Egypt*.

_____. "Carroll Recital Pleasant," *Los Angeles Times* (May 20, 1964). Review of performance of *Sonnets for Soprano and String Quartet*.

_____. "Choice Concert Stars Pelletier and [Leonard] Warren," *Los Angeles Times* (August 6, 1952). Review of *The Crystal Lake*.

_____. "International Night Features Nikolaidi," *Los Angeles Times* (March 4, 1955). Premiere of *Suite for Orchestra*.

_____. "L.A.'s 15th Festival of Music to Accent Moderns," *Los Angeles Times* (May 28, 1961).

_____. "Ojai Music Festival Holds Potent Appeal," *Los Angeles Times* (June 2, 1952). Review of *Singing Earth* premiere.

_____. "Patriotic Nostalgia at Bowl," *Los Angeles Times* (August 20, 1963). Review of premiere of *Our Beloved Land*.

_____. "Resident California Composers Honored," *Los Angeles Times* (April 30, 1963). Review of Royce Hall, UCLA, performance of *Sonnets for Soprano and String Orchestra*.

_____. "Warren Oratorio Well Sung By Wagner Chorus," *Los Angeles Times* (April 3, 1954). Review of 1954 performance of *The Passing of King Arthur*.

Goodland, Elizabeth. "Composer Elinor Remick Warren Brings Musical Honors to the City of Her Birth," *Los Angeles Times* (December 27, 1953). Announcement of Los Angeles Times "Woman of the Year" Award to Elinor Remick Warren, 1953.

Gowdy, Alma. "King Arthur Oratorio Conducted by Wagner," *Los Angeles Herald and Express* (April 3, 1954). Review of 1954 performance of *The Passing of King Arthur*.

_____. "Nikolaidi Thrills at Symphony," *Los Angeles Herald-Express* (March 4, 1955). Review of premiere of *Suite for Orchestra.*

Greene, Patterson. "A New Requiem," *Los Angeles Herald-Examiner* (April 3, 1966). Review of premiere of *Requiem.*

_____. "Elinor Warren Says American Composers in Vicious Circle," *Los Angeles Examiner* (July 29, 1951).

_____. "'Greats' Applaud Great Festival," *Los Angeles Examiner* (June 9, 1961). Review of world premiere of *Abram in Egypt.*

_____. "Jennie Tourel Wins Praise," *Los Angeles Examiner* (March 22, 1946). Review of *The Crystal Lake.*

_____. "*King Arthur* Gets Plaudits," *Los Angeles Examiner* (April 3, 1954). Review of 1954 performance of *The Passing of King Arthur.*

_____. "Ojai Festivals," *Los Angeles Examiner* (June 2, 1952). Review of *Singing Earth* premiere.

_____. "The Passing of Arthur," *Los Angeles Examiner* (March 29, 1954). Review of 1954 performance of *The Passing of King Arthur.*

_____. "Pelletier Excellent," *Los Angeles Examiner* (August 6, 1952). Review of *The Crystal Lake.*

_____. "Remick [Warren] *Suite* Merits Place," *Los Angeles Examiner* (March 4, 1955). Review of premiere of *Suite for Orchestra.*

_____. "Two Sacred Services," *Los Angeles Herald-Examiner* (April 4, 1966). Review of premiere of *Requiem.*

"Grete Stueckgold," *Musical Courier* (February 29, 1936). Review of recital, featuring group of Warren songs.

Gwin, Adrian, "Teens Pay Tribute to City Symphony," *Daily Mail* [Charleston, WV] (October 24, 1955). Review of *Along the Western Shore.*

Hall, Don Alan. "Choral Works Steal Thunder," *Gazette-Times* [Corvallis, OR] (May 24, 1979). Review of *Good Morning, America!*

Harford, Margaret. "Jennie Tourel Delightful in Local Debut," *Hollywood* [CA] *Citizen-News* (March 22, 1946). Review of *The Crystal Lake.*

Haynes, Alfred. "Symphony Excels in Warren Work," *The Evening Sun* [Baltimore, MD] (April 21, 1986). Review of performance of *Suite for Orchestra.*

Herreshoff, Constance. "Symphony Playing Tops First Concert," *San Diego* [CA] *Union* (August 8, 1951).

Hickman, C.S. "Concerts in Los Angeles," *Christian Science
Monitor* (date unknown). Review of *The Crystal Lake.*

____. "*Suite for Orchestra* First Performance," *Musical
Courier* (May 1955).

Howard, Orrin. "Serious Music Is Rarity for Women,"
Hollywood [CA] *Citizen-News* (April 1, 1966).

____. "Warren *Requiem* Given Premiere," *Hollywood* [CA]
Citizen-News (April 4, 1966). Review of premiere of
Requiem.

"John Barbirolli," *Pacific Coast Musician* (date unknown).
Review of *Intermezzo* from *The Passing of King
Arthur.*

Jones, Isabel Morse. "Evening of Romanticism Enjoyed at
Philharmonic," *Los Angeles Times* (March 22, 1946).
Review of *The Crystal Lake.*

____. "Kirsten Flagstad Sings Noteworthy Concert to Phil-
harmonic Throng," *Los Angeles Times* (May 4, 1938).
Review of Flagstad's singing of *Snow Towards
Evening.*

____. "Music Holds to Spirit of Good Friday," *Los Angeles
Times* (March 23, 1940). Review of premiere of *The
Passing of King Arthur.*

____. "Noteworthy Concert Given by Richard Crooks," *Los
Angeles Times* (April 12, 1939). Review of three Warren songs sung in this recital.

____. "Society of Composers Auspiciously Launched," *Los
Angeles Times* (May 26, 1937). Review of *Quintet for
Woodwinds.*

____. "Suite by Purcell Feature of Barbirolli's Program,"
Los Angeles Times (August 9, 1941). Review of *Intermezzo* from *The Legend of King Arthur.*

____. "The Week's High Note in Music," *Los Angeles
Times* (March 24, 1940). Review of premiere of *The
Passing of King Arthur.*

____. "Two Concerts Win Favor," *Los Angeles Times* (date
unknown). Review of *The Harp Weaver.*

Kendall, Raymond. "Nikolaidi Sparks International Night,"
Mirror-News [Los Angeles] (March 4, 1955). Review of
premiere of *Suite for Orchestra.*

____. "Ojai Stages Its Sixth Festival," *Los Angeles Mirror* (June 2, 1952). Review of *Singing Earth* premiere.

____. "Pelletier, [Leonard] Warren at Bowl Event," *Los Angeles Mirror* (August 6, 1952). Review of *The Crystal Lake.*

Kremenliev, B. Review of *Abram in Egypt*, Los Angeles, in *Musical Courier* (July, 1961).

Kutsky, Diana. "Composer Grateful to OSU [Oregon State University]," *Gazette-Times* [Corvallis, OR] (date unknown).

Lalaouni, Alexandra. "The State Orchestra Under Parides: American Compositions," *Vrathyni* [Athens, Greece] (July 29, 1955). Review of *Singing Earth.*

Lawrence, Florence. "Miss Warren's Chorale Earns Big Ovation," *Los Angeles Examiner* (March 22, 1940). Review of premiere of *The Passing of King Arthur.*

"L.A. Composer to Hear Premiere of Own Work," *Los Angeles Herald* (March 11, 1940).

"The Limelight," National Federation of Music Clubs *Music Clubs Magazine* (Winter, 1970-1971). Re: *Symphony in One Movement.*

"Local Composer Symphony Enthusiast," *Philharmonic Reporter* (program date unknown).

"Los Angeles Woman to Hear Premiere of Her Composition," *Los Angeles Times* (March 18, 1940).

M.L.S. "Elinor Remick Warren Has Busy Musical Life," *Musical Courier* (June, 1953).

Moffat, Frances. "The Perfect Score for a Marriage," *San Francisco Chronicle* (November 18, 1970).

Monson, Karen. "Composers Who Happen to Be Female," *Los Angeles Herald-Examiner* (May 21, 1972).

____. "Tribute to the Musical Sisterhood," *Los Angeles Herald-Examiner* (March 31, 1972).

Montgomery, Merle. "We're on the Air! It's Time to Tune In," National Federation of Music Clubs *Music Clubs Magazine* (Summer, 1972).

Morrow, Grace. "Many Women Composers Hold Academic Posts," *Abilene* [TX] *Reporter-News* (March 25, 1976).

Mort, Frances. "Musical Program Applauded," unidentified newspaper (July 15, 1939). Review of joint recital by Warren and Nadine Connor.

Morton, Rachel. "*Abram in Egypt* Premiered for Distinguished Audience," *Long Beach* [CA] *Independent* (June 9, 1961). Review of world premiere of *Abram in Egypt*.

_____. "L.A. Composer Hailed in Premiere of Work," *Long Beach* [CA] *News* (June 9, 1961). Review of world premiere of *Abram in Egypt*.

"Mother & Daughter: Griffins Create Piano Rhapsody," *Mirror-News* [Los Angeles] (date unknown).

"Mrs. Griffins's Wilshire District Home Reverberates with Music," unidentified newspaper (August 23, 1951).

"New Warren Compositions Heard," *Pacific Coast Musician* (January 17, 1942).

Nichols, Dorothy, "Mass, Modern Work Feature Program," *Palo Alto* [CA] *Times* (July 26, 1961). Review of *Abram in Egypt* at Stanford University.

_____. "Stanford Symphony Offers Varied, Romantic Concert," *Palo Alto* [CA] *Times* (December 7, 1970). Review of premiere of *Symphony in One Movement*.

Norcott, B.J. "Elinor Remick Warren: Marriage, Music, Magnetism," *Californian* (February, 1950).

Norton, Mildred. "Choral Work Wins Kudos All Round," *Los Angeles Daily News* (April 3, 1954). Review of 1954 performance of *The Passing of King Arthur*.

_____. "Hollywood Bowl," *Los Angeles Daily News* (August 6, 1952). Review of *The Crystal Lake*.

_____. Interview with Elinor Remick Warren, *Los Angeles Daily News* (September 18, 1951).

_____. "Music Review," *Los Angeles Daily News* (March 22, 1946). Review of *The Crystal Lake*.

_____. "Ojai Festivals," *Los Angeles Daily News* (June 2, 1952). Review of *Singing Earth* Premiere.

"Noted Tenor's Graciousness Wins Audience," newspaper unidentified (April 12, 1939). Review of a group of Warren songs sung by Richard Crooks.

"Occidental Degree for Elinor Warren," *Los Angeles Examiner* (June 22, 1954).

Passetti, Joyce. "Composing Is a Wonderful Career," *Palo Alto* [CA] *Times* (July 25, 1961).

"*The Passing of King Arthur: Intermezzo,* by Warren," *Standard School Broadcast* #15 (February 18, 1943). Commentary to accompany broadcast for school children.

Perlee, Charles D. "Feld Quartet in Top Form for Watchorn Hall Concert," *The Daily Sun* [Redlands, CA] (October 14, 1959). Review of *Sonnets for Soprano and String Quartet.*

_____. "'Strictly Highbrow' Concert Given by Quartet at Bowl," *The Daily Sun* [Redlands, CA] (August 3, 1960). Review of *Sonnets for Soprano and String Quartet.*

Peterson, Melody. "Many Women Wait to Be Liberated As Classical Composers," *Los Angeles Times* (date unknown).

"Philharmonic Recognizes Los Angeles Composer," *Los Angeles Times* (March 17, 1940).

Pike, Alberta. "Soprano Enthralls Audience," *Denver Post* (date unknown). Review of Kirsten Flagstad concert of Fall 1935, where she sang *White Horses of the Sea.*

Portser, Dorothy Virginia. "...Elinor Remick Warren's Symphonic Opus Finds Favor in Hollywood," *Enquirer* [New York] (March 25, 1940).

"Die Priesträger," *Mannheimer Morgen* [Mannheim, Germany] (August 16, 1961). Announcement, in German, of Gedok Prize to *Abram in Egypt.*

Princi, Carl. "Profile: Elinor Remick Warren," *KFAC Magazine* (November/December, 1976). With cover portrait drawing by Jan Jellins.

Quirk, Lucy. "Woman of the Month: Elinor Remick Warren," Southland Women's Clubs *Tableau* (November, 1947).

Robin, H. "Music of Our Time," *Musical America* (July, 1961). Re: premiere of *Abram in Egypt;* includes portrait (p. 10).

Rockwell. John. "Concert Salutes Distaff Composers," *Los Angeles Times* (May 29, 1972). Review of *Symphony in One Movement.*

Rodriguez, Jose. "Philharmonic Gets Second Coates," *Rob Wagner's Script* (March 30, 1940). Review of premiere of *The Passing of King Arthur.*

"Rose Bampton Here for Ojai Festival Concerts," *Los Angeles Times* (May 29, 1952).

Russell, Smith. "Los Angeles International Music Festival Impressive Success," *Music of the West* (July, 1961). Review of world premiere of *Abram in Egypt*.

S.T. de B. "Québec Symphony Orchestra Holds Final Concert Here," *Québec Chronicle-Telegraph* (May 9, 1955). Review of *Suite for Orchestra*.

Saltzberg, Geraldine. "Accomplished Composer's Youth Belies Her Musical Eminence," *Arizona Daily Star* (October 13, 1959).

_____. "Ricci Stars with Tucson Symphony," *Arizona Daily Star* (October 14, 1959). Review of *The Crystal Lake*.

"Saluting Women Conductors and Composers," National Federation of Music Clubs *Music Clubs Magazine* (Winter, 1976-1977). Re: *Abram in Egypt*; with illustration.

Sanborn, Pitts. Review of *The Harp Weaver*, *New York World-Telegram* (April 15, 1936).

Saunders, Richard D. "Amazing Performance: Meremblum Junior Orchestra Superb," *Hollywood* [CA] *Citizen-News* (January 15, 1962). Review of *The Fountain*.

_____. "Bowl Fans Applaud Barbirolli," *Hollywood* [CA] *Citizen-News* (August 9, 1941). Review of *Intermezzo* from *The Passing of King Arthur*.

_____. "California Composers' Festival," *Pacific Coast Musician* (June 5, 1937). Review of *Quintet for Woodwinds*.

_____. "Coates Paid Ovation for New Work," *Hollywood* [CA] *Citizen-News* (March 22, 1940). Review of premiere of *The Passing of King Arthur*.

_____. "Crooks Wins Ovation in Song Recital," *Hollywood* [CA] *Citizen-News* (April 12, 1939). Review of three Warren songs sung in this recital.

_____. "Gebert Scores in Concert," *Los Angeles Examiner* (November 26, 1958). Review of *The Crystal Lake*.

_____. "Hollywood Hears Premiere of Choral-Symphonic Poem," *Musical Courier* (date unknown). With cover photograph of Warren onstage with orchestra and chorus at premiere of *The Passing of King Arthur*.

____. "L.A. Woman Composer's *Passing of King Arthur* to Be Given," *The Citizen News* [Hollywood, CA] (March 14, 1940).

____. "New Warren Work Scores," *Los Angeles Examiner* (November 16, 1954).

____. "Recital Fans Again Praise Native Music," *Hollywood* [CA] *Citizen-News* (May 26, 1937). Review of *Quintet for Woodwinds*.

____. "Three Concerts Offered," *Hollywood* [CA] *Citizen-News* (August 11, 1941). Review of *The Harp Weaver*.

Schallert, Edwin. "Choral Symphonic Poem Given Premiere," *Los Angeles Times* (March 22, 1940). Review of premiere of *The Passing of King Arthur*.

Schallert, Elza. "Composer - With Glamour," *Los Angeles Times Sunday Magazine* (April 21, 1940).

Shippey, Lee. "Lee Side o' L.A.," *Los Angeles Times* (May 11, 1939). Article about Warren.

Smith, Anne T. "A Symphony of Home, Music," *Los Angeles Herald-Examiner* (date unknown).

Smith, Catherine Parsons, Ph.D. "Resident Composers in Southern California before 1935: The First Los Angeles School." Unpublished paper.

Smith, Julia. "Elinor Remick Warren Honored in Israel," National Federation of Music Clubs *Music Clubs Magazine* (Winter, 1976-1977).

Sonne, Ann. "Miss Warren Calm Over Debut of Her *Requiem*," *Los Angeles Times* (April 1, 1966).

Soucek, Carol. "Composer Warren: 'Family Came First,'" *Los Angeles Herald-Examiner* (September 12, 1974).

Sperer-Drakon, Lily. "A Concert by the Symphonic Orchestra with Modern American Compositions," *Athinaiki* [Athens, Greece] (July 27, 1955). Review of *Singing Earth*.

"Stanford to Honor Woman Composer," *Palo Alto* [CA] *Times* (July 24, 1961).

Sullivan, Edward S. "Variety Marks International Program at Philharmonic," newspaper unidentified (March 4, 1955). Review of premiere of *Suite for Orchestra*.

"Symphony, Chorus to Fete L.A. Composer," *San Francisco Chronicle* (July 25, 1961).

"Symphony Honors Native Los Angeles Composer," *Los Angeles Examiner* (March 17, 1940).

Taylor, Deems. Review of *The Harp Weaver*, *New York Evening World* (April 15, 1936).

Thackeray, Guy. "Symphony's New Model Fine One," *Tucson* [AZ] *Daily Star* (October 14, 1959). Review of *The Crystal Lake*.

"Three from CRI," *Musical America* (February, 1964). Review of recordings of *Abram in Egypt* and *Suite for Orchestra*.

"Times Woman of Year Given Music Honor," *Los Angeles Times* (June 15, 1954).

Toberman, Lucy. "Her Two 'Careers' - Music, Family," *Larchmont Chronicle* [Los Angeles] (August, 1969).

Townsend, Dorothy. "Music-Wise: L.A. Big Girl, Says Woman Composer," *Los Angeles Times* (June 1, 1961).

"Two to Perform in Recital at Hardin-Simmons University," *Abilene* [TX] *Reporter-News* (February 15, 1976).

Ussher, Bruno David. Review of Elinor Remick Warren's performance as piano soloist with the Los Angeles Philharmonic, *Saturday Night*, (January 30, 1926).

____. "Sounding Board," *Evening News* [Pasadena, CA] (March 16, 1940). Re: rehearsal of *The Passing of King Arthur*.

____. "Speaking of Music: The American Habit," *Pasadena* [CA] *Star-News* (March 23, 1940). Review of premiere of *The Passing of King Arthur*.

____. "Woman Composer Feted," *Evening News* [Pasadena, CA] (March 22, 1940). Review of premiere of *The Passing of King Arthur*.

Vokos, George. "Works by American Composers Performed by Our Symphonic Orchestra," *Akropolis* [Athens, Greece] (July 30, 1955). Review of *Singing Earth*.

W.S.T. "Elinor Remick Warren," Newspaper unidentified [Mannheim, Germany] (September, 1961). Announcement in German of Gedok Prize to *Abram in Egypt*.

Waldorf, Dolores. "Famous Woman Composer Irked by Comparisons," *Oakland* [CA] *Tribune* (July 25, 1961).

Warren, Elinor Remick. "The Distaff Side," *Music and Dance in Southern California* (1946).

_____. "Musician Combines Art, Home-Making," *The Mills Quarterly* [Mills College, Oakland, CA] (Winter, 1946).

"Warren *Suite* Wallenstein Premiere - Canadian Premiere, Pelletier," Sigma Alpha Iota *Pan Pipes* (January, 1956).

Wilke, Marion. "*Abram in Egypt* Tells in Song Dead Sea Scrolls Heroic Story," *Rockford* [IL] *Morning Star* (April 26, 1963).

_____. "Sudler Repeats Past Successes in Concert Here," *Rockford* [IL] *Register* (April 26, 1963). Review of *Abram in Egypt*.

Williams, Bessie K. "Native Music Gains Favor of Auditors," Newspaper unidentified (May 26, 1937). Review of *Quintet for Woodwinds*.

"Women Composers: En Route," *Musical America* (June, 1975). Survey of major symphony orchestras performing works by women composers during the decade 1965-75.

"Women Composers in Spotlight," *The Standard Star* [New Rochelle, NY] (February 19, 1969). Article about New York Public Library exhibit and concert honoring women composers.

Woods, Joan. "Her Fame's International: Concert Hall to Cattle Ranch," *San Francisco Examiner* (July 25, 1961).

"Works by Prokofieff, Warren, Foss, Tansman Introduced on West Coast," *Musical America* (date unknown). Review of premiere of *Suite for Orchestra*.

Zahl, Arne. "Anne Barrows Sparkles in Recital," *Press Telegram* [Long Beach, CA] (December 7, 1960). Review discusses performance of *Heather*.

INDEX